BRITAIN'S BEST

home cook

BRITAIN'S BEST
home cook
GREAT FOOD EVERY DAY

Foreword by
CLAUDIA WINKLEMAN

RECIPES BY JORDAN BOURKE
PHOTOGRAPHY BY KIM LIGHTBODY

BBC
BOOKS

CONTENTS

FOREWORD

I'll be completely honest: they had me at 'Mary'. That was all it took.
I didn't ask if it was a programme about the history of the avocado
(I would totally do that) or the new way to cut kiwi fruit (maybe less so),
but I was in. Mary is our absolute favourite at home; we never miss one
of her shows. My sister is her biggest fan and was cooking her recipes
thirty years ago.

'Britain's Best Home Cook' follows our three masterful judges – Mary,
the absolute expert on home cooking; Dan, edible and unbelievably
talented chef; and Chris, adorable and quite simply the king of all
produce – as they set brilliant cooking tasks for our ten fantastic cooks.

I'm going to be frank here. I thought home cooking was making toast
and heating soup. That's, um, my forte, you see. I thought it might be
'have a couple of hours to try and make a terrific egg sandwich and then
we'll all have a bite and relax'. That's what I'd assumed. That's what was
in my head.

Instead, these magnificent ten blew my tiny mind. They made dishes
that were so delicious I sometimes had to have a lie-down. I chased
them round the studio asking for recipes. (Fortunately, with this handy
cookbook, you don't have to do that.) Unlike other shows, there was
nothing fancy asked of them, nothing was served with a *jus* (still not sure
what that is). Instead, our cooks took extremely humble ingredients and,
with masterly skills, turned them into, quite simply, the tastiest food
I've ever had. Some cod and some cumin? Make a great dish out of an
aubergine? I was gobsmacked by the meals they produced.

We really hope you like this book. The recipes are easy (and if I'm saying
that, it means something) and freakishly yummy. If you don't like anything,
please call me and we can discuss. I live with Mary now; we'll be happy
to drop by.

Claudia Winkleman

INTRODUCTION

The BBC series 'Britain's Best Home Cook' is a celebration of the delicious food being cooked in households all over the UK today. There has never been a more exciting time to be a home cook, with superb-quality ingredients available everywhere, from delis and superstores to local markets and farm-to-fork delivery services. We all have our family favourites – dishes that remind us of home, meals we share with loved ones, classics we return to again and again, and recipes we hand down the generations. Britain's home cooks are inventive and inspiring and 'Britain's Best Home Cook' sets out to test the best.

This official book to accompany the BBC show brings together the most outstanding recipes from the series, with a collection of appetising and inspiring dishes with modern twists to go alongside. The imagination and culinary flair that went into the food created by the ten contestants was remarkable, demonstrating the immense talent of these cooks, who gave us their personal takes on well-loved dishes, celebrating their own cultural identities and backgrounds – a true representation of modern Britain.

The recipes accompanied by a 'Best of Home Cook' pot motif were selected to be featured from the show. Some recipes were adapted and simplified to make them accessible for cooks with the most basic kitchen equipment, to ensure fantastic results. All the recipes were tested and checked with the home cook in mind, ensuring that they are practical and achievable for everyone, and use ingredients that are readily available. Where a more unusual ingredient is integral to the dish, I have suggested alternatives that are easier to find, while staying true to the original contestant recipe. Tips are included throughout the book to give you ideas for easy variations or how to make a recipe vegetarian or vegan, so you can truly make each dish your own.

Britain's Best Home Cook is the ultimate British cooking companion, giving you the tools and knowledge to make timeless, delicious food at home – with classics such as Beef Wellington (page 184), Lancashire Hotpot (page 169) or a sumptuous Fish Pie (page 202) – including clear

step-by-step instructions to ensure a perfect dish every time. There are also plenty of dishes inspired by the cuisines that we Brits love, whether it's Jollof Rice (page 118), Chicken Biryani (page 122) or Sweet-and-Sour Pork (page 162), you'll find them here.

I hope *Britain's Best Home Cook* inspires you to get into the kitchen, even if you've never cooked a meal from scratch before (classic Sausages with Horseradish Mash (page 161) or Fish Butties (page 190) would be a great place to start). It's easy to get into a rut with cooking and find oneself making the same few meals again and again, but I hope the BBC series and this book will encourage you to mix up your home cooking and try out new dishes. Cooking and eating together are truly among life's great pleasures. And there's nothing like trying a new dish to get conversation going around the family kitchen table!

Britain's Best Home Cook is a book you will return to day after day, whether you are looking for a light soup or salad, a fiery curry, a hearty pie or some comforting pasta. There are sweet tarts, indulgent puddings and impress-your-friends cakes – something for every mood and occasion. So, if you've seen something on the show that inspires you, look it up and get into the kitchen!

Jordan Bourke

LIGHT BITES

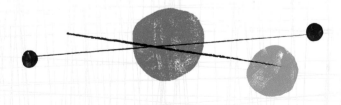

POACHED EGGS WITH HOLLANDAISE & ASPARAGUS ON SOURDOUGH

A classic start to a leisurely weekend morning: it is hard to beat poached eggs and asparagus bathed in hollandaise sauce.

Serves 2
Prep time: 10 minutes
Cook time: 25 minutes
VEGETARIAN

150g (5oz) asparagus spears,
    woody ends snapped off
2 eggs
2 slices of sourdough bread
salted butter
sea salt and black pepper

For the hollandaise sauce
2 egg yolks
120g (4½oz) unsalted butter, diced
2 tsp fresh lemon juice
1 tbsp cold water
a few ice cubes (optional)

1. For the hollandaise, put the egg yolks, butter, lemon juice and water into a heavy-based pan and place over the lowest possible heat. If you do not have a heavy-based pan, put the ingredients in a heatproof bowl over a pan of barely simmering water, ensuring the base of the bowl does not come into contact with the water. Using a balloon whisk, immediately begin whisking until the butter has melted and has combined with the egg yolks and liquid. Do not increase the heat or stop whisking at any point, and make sure the sides of your pan are never too hot to touch.

2. Once the butter has completely melted, turn up the heat ever so slightly and keep whisking continuously until the sauce has thickened. If the sauce starts to split, it means the heat is too high: drop in an ice cube and whisk until it comes back together and thickens. Transfer the sauce to a bowl and set aside.

3. Bring a pan of salted water to the boil and cook the asparagus in the boiling water for 2 minutes until just tender and still emerald green. Remove with a slotted spoon, rinse under cold running water and set aside. Reduce the heat to the lowest setting, until the water is barely simmering: there should be no bubbling or movement in the water at all. Crack the eggs into a cup and gently lower towards the water, tipping out the eggs. Cook for 3–5 minutes, until the whites have set and the yolks are cooked to your liking. Remove and drain on kitchen paper.

4. Toast the bread and slather with salted butter. Top with the asparagus and poached eggs. Whisk the hollandaise until smooth. If you want your sauce a little thinner, whisk in a teaspoon or two of boiling water. Dollop the hollandaise over the eggs, season with salt and pepper and serve immediately.

CHARRED LEEKS, SOFT-BOILED EGGS & BASIL OIL

Blanching and roasting the leeks makes them really tender and delicious. They could also be served on their own as a side dish.

Serves 4
Prep time: 10 minutes
Cook time: 25 minutes
VEGETARIAN

6 leeks
4 eggs
2 tbsp olive oil
4 thick slices of sourdough bread
a handful of basil leaves
1 garlic clove, crushed
5 tbsp extra-virgin olive oil
1 tsp dried chilli flakes
sea salt and black pepper

1. Preheat the oven to 200°C/180°C fan/gas 6 and bring a large pan of salted water to the boil.

2. Trim the leeks, but don't take too much off the root end. Add the leeks and the eggs to the boiling water. Cook the leeks for 4–5 minutes until barely tender, then remove and drain well on kitchen paper or a clean tea towel. Continue to cook the eggs for another 2 minutes: they should have no more than 6 minutes in total. Immediately transfer the eggs to a bowl of cold water and refresh until they have cooled but are still warm.

3. Put the drained leeks in a roasting tin, drizzle over the two tablespoons of olive oil, season well with salt and pepper and bake for 15–20 minutes until golden and crisp on the outside. Remove and cut the leeks in half lengthways.

4. Meanwhile, toast the bread and finely chop the basil. In a bowl, combine the basil with the garlic, extra-virgin olive oil and a pinch of salt. Peel the eggs and slice in half.

5. To serve, divide the toasted sourdough among serving plates, drizzle some of the basil oil over the sourdough, top with the leeks and eggs, and finish with the remaining basil oil and the chilli flakes scattered over. Serve immediately.

SCOTCH EGGS

Scotch eggs are just as delicious eaten at room temperature as they are straight out of the oven. Perfect for a picnic or for a decadent lunch box, and even better served with tartare sauce.

Best of
HOME
COOK

Makes 4 Scotch eggs
Prep time: 25 minutes
Cook time: 20–25 minutes

5 eggs
4 pork sausages, about 275g (10oz)
20g (¾oz) chives, finely chopped
20g (¾oz) flat-leaf parsley leaves,
    finely chopped
pinch of freshly grated nutmeg
1 tsp English mustard
100g (4oz) plain flour
100g (4oz) fresh white breadcrumbs
400ml (14fl oz) vegetable oil
sea salt and black pepper

For the tartare sauce
200g (7oz) mayonnaise
2 tbsp cornichons, finely chopped
1 tbsp capers, chopped
2 spring onions, finely chopped
2 tsp Dijon mustard
1 tbsp fresh lemon juice

1. To make the tartare sauce, mix everything together in a bowl and set aside.

2. Bring a pan of water to the boil. Gently lower four of the eggs into the water, bring back up to the boil, then simmer for 7 minutes. Transfer to a bowl of iced water and leave to cool for a few minutes, then carefully peel.

3. Preheat the oven to 190°C/170°C fan/gas 5.

4. Squeeze the sausages out of their skins and into a bowl. Add the chives, parsley, nutmeg, mustard, half a teaspoon of salt and a good grinding of black pepper. Mix well.

5. Beat the remaining egg in a bowl. Put the flour and breadcrumbs in separate bowls.

6. Divide the sausage meat into four equal pieces and flatten each piece into a thin oval-shaped patty. Roll the peeled eggs in the flour and sit one on top of each patty. Gently mould the meat around the eggs, shaping with your hands until even and sealed.

7. Roll the meat-wrapped eggs in the flour, shake off any excess, then dip into the beaten egg, and finally roll in the breadcrumbs until evenly covered. For an extra-thick coating, roll them in the egg and breadcrumbs a second time.

8. Heat the oil in a large deep pan. Carefully lower the eggs into the oil and cook for 4–6 minutes, turning occasionally, until crisp and golden. Remove using a slotted spoon and drain on kitchen paper. Place in a small roasting tin and bake for 10 minutes.

9. Remove from the oven and leave to cool for 10 minutes before serving with the tartare sauce.

SMOKED MACKEREL PÂTÉ WITH CAPERS ON RYE

A good mackerel pâté makes a wonderful starter, snack or canapé.
To make canapés, toast the bread, then stamp out little rounds using
a small pastry cutter or cut the toast into small squares. Pile on the
pâté, capers, dill and cress and serve with some lemon wedges.

Serves 4
Prep time: 10 minutes

250g (9oz) smoked mackerel fillets
100g (4oz) cream cheese
100g (4oz) crème fraîche
1 tsp freshly grated horseradish or
    creamed horseradish from a jar
1 tsp Dijon mustard
1 lemon: grated zest
    of ½ and 2–3 tbsp juice
sea salt and black pepper

To serve
4 slices of rye or other
    good-quality bread
salted butter
1 tbsp capers
small handful of dill fronds
small handful of salad cress
lemon wedges (optional)

1. Peel the skin off the mackerel and check for any little bones. Put the flesh into a food processor together with the cream cheese, crème fraîche, horseradish, mustard, lemon zest and two tablespoons of the lemon juice. Pulse until you have a rough texture. If you prefer it completely smooth, you can continue to pulse, but a bit of texture is rather nice. Season to taste with salt and pepper and little more lemon juice if necessary.

2. Toast the bread and spread with a little butter. Serve it with the pâté, scattered with the capers, dill and salad cress. Serve lemon wedges on the side, if you wish.

Tip
Smoked mackerel is readily available, but you might like to try hot-smoking your own fish. There are lots of simple and inexpensive home-smokers available to buy (try online or in good kitchen shops), or you can improvise one at home by fitting a baking rack into a large heavy-based pan with a tight-fitting lid. You will also need some non-resinous wood chips or sawdust (look online). The best woods for mackerel or other oily fish are extra-fine beech or alder chips, which are smoky and slightly sweet. Make sure your kitchen is well ventilated.

Scatter a good layer of sea salt on a plate, place fresh mackerel fillets on top and cover with another good layer of salt. Leave for 5–10 minutes, to draw off moisture, then thoroughly rinse and pat dry with kitchen paper. Put the wood chips in the bottom of your smoker, or pan, pop on the lid and place over a high heat. When the wood starts smouldering, turn the heat to low, put the fish fillets on the rack, replace the lid and cook for 5–10 minutes, until the flesh is opaque and flakes easily.

GIN-CURED TROUT WITH FENNEL SLAW & BEETROOT WEDGES

Curing the trout with gin, sugar and salt gives the fish a firm texture and a lovely fresh flavour. You can cure the fish a day ahead, but do not leave it in the mixture for more than 50 minutes or the flesh will become too salty and sweet.

Serves 2
Prep time: 20 minutes
Cook time: 40 minutes

100ml (3½fl oz) gin
50g (2oz) fine sea salt
50g (2oz) caster sugar
250g (9oz) very fresh (sushi grade)
    trout fillet
2 small raw beetroot
2 tbsp olive oil
1 fennel bulb
3 tbsp crème fraîche
1 tbsp Dijon mustard
grated zest of ½ lemon
sea salt and black pepper
a few dill fronds, to serve

1. Put the gin, salt and sugar in a pan over a medium heat. Gently warm the mixture, stirring all the time, until the sugar and salt have dissolved. Ensure it does not come to the boil. Remove from the heat and leave to cool completely, then chill in the fridge.

2. Remove the skin from the trout and cut the flesh into thin slices, similar to sushi or sashimi. Add the sliced trout to the chilled gin mixture, turn to coat and leave to cure for no more than 50 minutes at room temperature. Drain, discarding the marinade liquid, and rinse the fish under cold water, pat dry and keep in the fridge until ready to serve.

3. Preheat the oven to 200°c/180°c fan/gas 6.

4. Top and tail the beetroot, but do not peel. Cut in half and then into 2cm (¾in) wedges. Put them into a roasting tin, toss with the olive oil and season with salt and pepper. Roast for 30–35 minutes or until tender and the skins are beginning to blister. Leave to cool to room temperature.

5. Very thinly slice the fennel, using a mandoline if you have one. Transfer to a bowl, combine with the crème fraîche, mustard and lemon zest and season to taste with salt and pepper.

6. To serve, put the fennel onto a plate and top with the beetroot wedges and cured trout. Scatter over the dill and serve immediately.

Best of
HOME
COOK

ULTIMATE GRUYÈRE, CHEDDAR & SAGE TOASTIES

The marriage of Gruyère and Cheddar with sage makes for a heavenly cheese toastie. The bread here is important: something fairly robust like sourdough or a white bloomer is best for frying and soaking up all the delicious flavours.

Serves 4
Prep time: 5 minutes
Cook time: 10 minutes
VEGETARIAN

salted butter, softened
8 slices of sourdough bread
   or white bloomer
150g (5oz) mature Cheddar, grated
120g (4½oz) Gruyère, grated
16 fresh sage leaves

1. Heat a flat griddle pan or heavy-based frying pan over a medium–low heat.

2. Butter both sides of all eight slices of bread. Divide the grated cheese between four of them. Top each with four of the sage leaves and place the remaining bread on top to create a sandwich. Press down firmly.

3. Place as many sandwiches as will fit into your pan and fry for 4–5 minutes on each side until crisp and golden and the cheese has melted on the inside. Serve immediately.

GRILLED THAI PRAWNS

The Thai-style sauce for these prawns is a perfect balance of sweet, sour and salty. Do not add the prawns to the lime juice mix more than 5 minutes before you intend to cook the dish, as the lime juice will make the prawns rubbery.

Serves 2
Prep time: 10 minutes
Cook time: 6–7 minutes

20g fresh coriander leaves
grated zest of 1 lemon
3 garlic cloves, crushed
3 tbsp fresh lime juice
1 tbsp fish sauce
1 tbsp soft brown sugar
1 tbsp sunflower oil
12 large raw tiger prawns,
    shell on

1. Finely chop the coriander (reserving a few leaves for garnish if desired) and add to a bowl with the remaining ingredients.

2. Set a pan over a high heat and, once hot, add the prawns and lime juice mixture and cook for 3–4 minutes, turning the prawns halfway, until they are cooked through. Remove the prawns and cook the liquid for another 3 minutes until reduced.

3. Arrange the prawns on a serving plate and drizzle with the sauce. Scatter over the reserved coriander leaves, if you wish. Serve immediately, with an extra bowl on the side for the discarded shells, and plenty of napkins.

Tip
To turn this into a more substantial meal, peel the prawns before cooking and serve with cooked jasmine rice.

SAUSAGE ROLLS

Home-made flaky pastry has an unbeatable texture and flavour, and it is quite straightforward to make. However, if you are really stuck for time, you can use good-quality shop-bought puff pastry instead.

Makes 18–20 sausage rolls
Prep time: 45 minutes,
    plus 30 minutes chilling
Cook time: 35–40 minutes

For the filling
300g (10½oz) minced pork: shoulder
    and belly (ask at your local
    butcher or the meat counter
    of your supermarket)
100g (4oz) smoked streaky bacon
    or pancetta, very finely chopped
25g (1oz) fresh breadcrumbs
1 tbsp fresh thyme leaves
2 tsp chopped sage leaves
fine sea salt and black pepper
piccalilli, chutney or other
    condiments, to serve

For the pastry
160g (5½oz) plain flour, plus extra
    for dusting
¼ tsp fine sea salt
100g (4oz) unsalted butter, chilled
    and cut into small pieces
2–2½ tablespoons water
1 egg, beaten

1. For the pastry, put the flour and salt into the bowl of a food processor. Add the chilled butter and blitz until it resembles fine breadcrumbs. Alternatively, rub the butter into the flour using your fingertips. Add the water and use your hands to bring the dough together until it forms a smooth ball. If it is still crumbly, add a few drops of water at a time, being careful not to overdo it. Shape the pastry into a narrow oblong, wrap in clingfilm and refrigerate for 30 minutes.

2. Preheat the oven to 200°C/180°C fan/gas 6. Line one or two baking sheets with baking parchment.

3. For the filling, put the pork, bacon, breadcrumbs and herbs into a bowl and season with three-quarters of a teaspoon of salt and half a teaspoon of freshly ground black pepper. Thoroughly combine together until evenly mixed: the best way to do this is using your hands.

4. Dust your work surface lightly with flour. Roll out the pastry into a long rectangle, roughly 12cm (5in) wide and 5mm (¼in) thick. Roll out the pork mixture into a long sausage shape, to the same length as your pastry rectangle. Place the pork mixture along the left-hand side of the pastry. Brush the right-hand side with beaten egg, then roll the left side of the pastry over onto the right, encasing the pork mixture. Seal the edge of the pastry by pressing with your fingers or the back of a fork. Brush some beaten egg over the pastry, then slice into evenly sized sausage rolls. Transfer to the lined baking sheet/s and bake for 35–40 minutes until golden.

5. Leave to cool slightly before serving, with any condiments you like.

CHICKEN SKEWERS & CHINESE BROCCOLI

These skewers are a Chinese street food classic and perfect for when you have friends over for drinks, or as a delicious dinner served with rice.

Serves 4 (makes 12 skewers)
Prep time: 15 minutes,
    plus 1 hour (minimum)
    marinating
Cook time: 10 minutes

4 chicken breast fillets, cut into 3cm
    (about 1in) pieces
1 tbsp light soy sauce
1 tsp grated fresh root ginger
2 garlic cloves, crushed
1 tbsp caster sugar
1 tbsp mirin
1 tbsp sake or dry sherry
½ tsp sea salt and a grinding
    of black pepper
2 tbsp finely snipped fresh chives

For the Chinese broccoli
1 tbsp groundnut oil
250g (9oz) tenderstem broccoli
3 tbsp water
1 tbsp oyster sauce
1 tsp sesame oil
1 tsp light soy sauce
pinch of white pepper

1. Put the chicken into a bowl with all the other ingredients except the chives, stir to combine, cover and leave to marinate in the refrigerator for at least 1 hour.

2. When ready to cook, place a griddle pan over a medium heat. Thread the chicken onto 12 skewers. Cook the skewers on the griddle pan for 8–10 minutes, turning now and again, until cooked through.

3. While the chicken is cooking, prepare the broccoli. Heat the groundnut oil in a large pan (with a lid) over a high heat. Once hot, add the broccoli and water, cover with the lid and cook for 3 minutes. Remove the lid and fry for another 3 minutes, shaking the pan now and again. Remove from the heat and toss with the oyster sauce, sesame oil, soy sauce and pepper. Serve immediately, along with the chicken skewers, with the chives scattered over.

Best of
HOME
COOK

CRAB CAKES

Light, fresh and easy to make, these crab cakes are perfect as a starter. The fresh coriander chutney really brings the dish together.

Serves 4–6 (makes 20 crab cakes)
Prep time: 20 minutes, plus chilling
Cook time: 15 minutes

300g (10½oz) fresh white crab meat
1 shallot, finely chopped
1 garlic clove, crushed
small handful of flat-leaf parsley
    leaves, finely chopped
small handful of coriander leaves,
    finely chopped
½ tsp ground coriander
1 fresh red chilli, de-seeded and
    finely chopped
60g (2½oz) manchego cheese, grated
1 tbsp fresh lemon juice
50g (2oz) fresh breadcrumbs
4 tbsp mayonnaise
50g (2oz) plain flour
1 egg, beaten
60g (2½oz) panko breadcrumbs,
    or extra fresh breadcrumbs
vegetable oil for frying
sea salt and black pepper
150g (5oz) rocket, to serve

For the coriander chutney
25g (1oz) fresh coriander,
    including stalks
6 tbsp extra-virgin olive oil
1 tbsp fresh lemon juice
½ fresh red or green chilli, de-seeded
    (optional)

1. Squeeze any excess liquid out of the crab meat. Add the crab to a bowl, together with the shallot, garlic, fresh parsley and coriander, the ground coriander, chilli, cheese, lemon juice, breadcrumbs and mayonnaise. Season to taste with salt and pepper and mix until well combined. Divide the mixture into 20 equal portions and form into slightly flattened balls. Refrigerate for 15 minutes.

2. For the coriander chutney, put all the ingredients into a food processor and blitz to a rough paste. Season to taste with salt; set aside.

3. Put the flour, beaten egg and breadcrumbs in separate bowls.

4. Coat the chilled crab cakes in the flour, then in the beaten egg, and finally roll in the panko (or fresh) breadcrumbs until evenly covered.

5. Fill a large deep heavy-based pan with oil to a depth of 2cm (¾in) and place over a medium–high heat. Test the oil is hot enough by dropping in a small piece of bread: it should brown in about 40 seconds. Carefully place the crab cakes in the oil, in batches, and fry for 3 minutes on each side until crisp and golden. Remove using a slotted spoon and drain on kitchen paper.

6. Serve the crab cakes with the rocket, with the coriander chutney drizzled over.

Best of
HOME
COOK

FALAFEL BITES

These wholesome patties can be served as a salad, or stuffed into pitta bread for a sandwich.

Serves 4 (makes about 30 falafel)
Prep time: 45 minutes, plus
    overnight soaking, plus chilling
Cook time: 10–15 minutes
VEGETARIAN
VEGAN

150g (5oz) dried chickpeas,
    soaked overnight
120g (4½oz) dried split broad beans,
    soaked overnight
4 garlic cloves
½ red onion, roughly chopped
15g (½oz) fresh coriander leaves
20g (¾oz) fresh parsley leaves
3 tbsp plain flour
1 tsp ground cumin
½ tsp smoked paprika
½ tsp baking powder
sunflower or vegetable oil, for frying
fine sea salt and black pepper

To serve
12–16 cherry tomatoes, halved
200g (7oz) rocket or other
    salad leaves
1 tbsp extra-virgin olive oil, plus
    extra to drizzle
1 tsp balsamic vinegar
hummus
4 pitta bread (optional)

1. Drain the soaked chickpeas and broad beans. In batches, add them to a food processor together with the garlic, onion, herbs, flour, spices, baking powder and half a teaspoon of salt. Blitz until everything is very finely chopped and almost smooth. If the mixture does not hold together when pressed between your fingers, blitz again until it does. Using your hands, take about two teaspoons of the mixture at a time and firmly press into small patties. Place on a tray and refrigerate for 20 minutes.

2. Fill a large deep heavy-based pan with oil to a depth of 2.5cm (1in) and place over a medium–high heat. Test the oil is hot enough by dropping in a small piece of bread: it should brown in 40–50 seconds. Add the falafel in batches: don't overcrowd the pan as it will bring the temperature down. Fry for 4–5 minutes, turning now and again, until golden brown and crisp on both sides. Remove and drain on kitchen paper. Keep warm while you cook the remaining falafel.

3. Toss the tomatoes, rocket, oil and vinegar together in a bowl and season with salt and pepper to taste. Plate up the salad with the falafel and hummus on top and drizzle with a little more olive oil. Alternatively, toast the pitta bread and stuff it with the salad, falafel and hummus.

Tip
Traditionally, falafel are made with a mixture of chickpeas and split broad beans; the latter can be found online and in some Middle Eastern shops. If you cannot find them, these are just as delicious made with chickpeas alone, substituting extra dried chickpeas for the beans.

SPICED CAULIFLOWER FRITTERS WITH YOGHURT DIP

Blending the onion, garlic and spices into the batter creates a deliciously moreish coating for the cauliflower.

Best of
HOME
COOK

Serves 4
Prep time: 10 minutes
Cook time: 15 minutes
VEGETARIAN

1 cauliflower, cut into small florets
1 tsp ground turmeric
120g (4½oz) gram flour
60g (2½oz) rice flour
1 tsp ground cumin
1 tsp garam masala
1 tsp fennel seeds
1 onion, peeled and quartered
3 garlic cloves, peeled
1 fresh red chilli, de-seeded
150ml (¼ pint) cold water
olive oil for frying
sea salt and black pepper

For the yoghurt dip
juice of 1 lime
150g (5oz) natural yoghurt
½ tsp caster sugar
a handful of mint leaves,
    roughly chopped

1. Bring a large pan of salted water to the boil and put the cauliflower in to cook, along with the turmeric. Reduce the heat and simmer for 3–4 minutes until barely tender. Drain thoroughly and return to the hot pan to dry out.

2. Put the gram flour and half a teaspoon of salt into a bowl and mix together. Add the cooked cauliflower and toss gently to coat.

3. For the yoghurt dip, combine the lime juice, yoghurt, sugar and most of the mint in a bowl. Season to taste and set aside.

4. For the batter, put the rice flour, cumin, garam masala, fennel seeds, onion, garlic and chilli into a food processor and blitz until finely ground. Slowly pour in the water and continue to blitz until you have a loose batter.

5. Pour the batter into the bowl of cauliflower and gently combine until evenly coated.

6. Heat three tablespoons of olive oil in a large non-stick frying pan over a medium heat. Once hot, add half the battered cauliflower and fry for 5–7 minutes, turning now and again, until golden and crisp on all sides. Remove using a slotted spoon and drain on kitchen paper. Add a few more tablespoons of olive oil to the pan and, when hot, fry the remaining cauliflower.

7. Scatter the reserved mint over the fritters and serve hot, with the yoghurt dip.

Tip
Gram flour is also known as chickpea flour or besan: it's available in larger supermarkets and in Indian stores. If you don't have rice flour you can use the same amount of plain flour.

CELERIAC & APPLE SOUP
WITH CRISPY BACON

Celeriac has a subtle, earthy, slightly nutty flavour, not quite as strong
as celery. It is perfectly matched with sweet apple and salty bacon.
Some apples can be a little more tart than others; if necessary, add
a teaspoon or two of sugar to balance that out (don't overdo it).

Serves 6
Prep time: 10 minutes,
    plus cooling
Cook time: 30–35 minutes
VEGETARIAN– omitting the bacon;
    see tip

3 tbsp olive oil
2 onions, finely chopped
1 litre (1¾ pints) water
100ml (3½fl oz) dry white wine
3 apples, peeled, cored and chopped
    into small cubes
600g (1lb 5oz) celeriac, peeled and
    roughly chopped into small cubes
¼ tsp freshly grated nutmeg
¼ tsp ground cinnamon
6 rashers rindless smoked
    streaky bacon
small handful of flat-leaf
    parsley leaves
sea salt and black pepper

1. Heat the oil in a large pan over a medium heat. Add the
onions and gently cook for 10 minutes until translucent.

2. Add the water, wine, apples and celeriac, bring to the boil,
then reduce the heat and simmer for 15–20 minutes until the
celeriac is soft. Remove from the heat and leave to cool for
about 10 minutes.

3. Using a blender or food processor, purée the mixture until
completely smooth, then return to the pan and place over a low
heat. Stir in the nutmeg and cinnamon and season to taste with
up to two teaspoons of salt and some pepper.

4. Meanwhile, fry the bacon until crisp, drain and cut into
small pieces.

5. To serve, ladle the soup into bowls and top with the bacon
and parsley.

Tip
If you are vegetarian, omit the bacon and replace with some
roasted nuts.

THAI CHICKEN COCONUT SOUP

This aromatic soup is surprisingly simple and quick to make. It is also a good dish to make the day before you plan on eating it, as the flavours intensify over time. Leave it to cool completely, cover and refrigerate, then reheat when ready to serve.

Serves 4–6
Prep time: 15 minutes
Cook time: 35 minutes

1 tbsp sunflower oil
1 onion, finely chopped
3 fresh red chillies, halved
    lengthways, de-seeded
    and finely sliced
3 garlic cloves, crushed
800ml (28fl oz) chicken stock
400ml (14fl oz) coconut milk
5cm (2in) piece of fresh galangal
    or root ginger, peeled and
    thinly sliced
5 fresh kaffir lime leaves
3 tbsp fish sauce
2 tsp caster sugar
2 sticks of lemongrass,
    halved lengthways
400g (14oz) boneless skinless chicken
    thighs, cut into small pieces
a handful of coriander leaves
2 limes, cut into wedges

1. Heat the oil in a large deep pan over a medium heat. Add the onion and most of the chilli and gently cook for 10 minutes until the onion is translucent. Add the garlic and cook for another 2 minutes until fragrant.

2. Add the stock, coconut milk, galangal or ginger, lime leaves, fish sauce, sugar and lemongrass. Bring to the boil and cook for 5 minutes, then reduce the heat, add the chicken pieces and gently simmer for 15 minutes until the chicken is cooked through.

3. To serve, stir in most of the coriander leaves, then remove the lemongrass and ladle into bowls. Scatter the remaining chilli and the coriander leaves on top and serve with lime wedges to squeeze over.

Tip
You can use prawns instead of chicken, if you prefer: add them to the soup after 10 minutes and simmer for a further 5 minutes.

BEETROOT SOUP WITH CUMIN-SPICED CHICKPEAS

Roasting raw beetroot gives this soup a wonderfully deep flavour, but if you are stuck for time you can use pre-cooked beetroot, which is easy to find in supermarkets – just ensure you don't buy the type packed in vinegar (see tip).

Serves 6
Prep time: 10 minutes,
    plus cooling
Cook time: 1 hour
VEGETARIAN – if made with
    vegetable stock

800g (1¾lb) raw beetroot
5 tbsp olive oil
300g (10½oz) cherry tomatoes
2 tbsp balsamic vinegar
2 onions, finely chopped
4 garlic cloves, crushed
1 litre (1¾ pints) chicken or
    vegetable stock
1 tsp ground cumin
1 × 400g tin chickpeas, drained
    and rinsed
1 tsp cumin seeds
sea salt and black pepper

To serve
natural yoghurt
small handful of flat-leaf parsley
    leaves, roughly chopped
extra-virgin olive oil

1. Preheat the oven to 200°C/180°C fan/gas 6.

2. Trim the beetroot (no need to peel) and slice into thin wedges. Put them into a roasting tin, toss with two tablespoons of the olive oil, one teaspoon of salt and a grinding of pepper. Cover with foil and bake for 30 minutes.

3. Add the tomatoes and balsamic vinegar. Replace the foil and bake for another 20 minutes until the beetroot is cooked through.

4. Meanwhile, heat two tablespoons of the olive oil in a large pan over a medium heat. Add the onions and gently cook for 10 minutes until translucent. Add the garlic and cook for another 2 minutes until fragrant.

5. When the beetroot and tomatoes are cooked, add them to the onions, together with the stock and ground cumin. Bring to the boil, then reduce the heat and simmer for 10 minutes. Leave to cool for 10 minutes, then purée using a blender or food processor. Taste and adjust the seasoning if necessary.

6. Heat the remaining one tablespoon of olive oil in a pan over a high heat. Add the chickpeas and fry for 3 minutes until golden and crisp. Add the cumin seeds and fry for another minute. Remove from the heat and season with salt and pepper.

7. Ladle the soup into bowls, top with a spoonful of yoghurt, fried chickpeas, parsley and a drizzle of extra-virgin olive oil.

Tip
If using pre-cooked beetroot, simply roast the tomatoes with the balsamic vinegar for 20 minutes before adding them to the pan with the onions, stock and beetroot.

SPICED BUTTERNUT SQUASH SOUP

This is the ultimate warming soup for a cold winter's day. The vegetable crisps give a delicious crunch, but add them just before serving, otherwise they will lose their bite.

Serves 4–6
Prep time: 15 minutes,
    plus cooling
Cook time: 35 minutes
VEGETARIAN – if made with
    vegetable stock

2 tbsp unsalted butter
2 tbsp olive oil
2 onions, finely chopped
1 fresh red or green chilli, de-seeded
    and finely chopped (optional)
5 garlic cloves, crushed
1 tsp curry powder
1¼ tsp smoked paprika
1 large butternut or onion squash
    (about 1kg/2¼lb), peeled,
    de-seeded and chopped
1 cooking apple, peeled, cored and
    roughly chopped
1 litre (1¾ pints) chicken or
    vegetable stock
sea salt and black pepper

To garnish
extra-virgin olive oil
vegetable crisps
1 tbsp snipped fresh chives

1. Heat the butter and olive oil in a large heavy-based pan over a low heat. Add the onions, chilli, garlic, curry powder and paprika and cook for 10 minutes, until the onions are translucent. If your onions and garlic begin to colour or burn, the heat is too high. Season with one teaspoon of salt and add the squash and apple. Continue to cook for 10 minutes, stirring occasionally to prevent sticking.

2. Pour in the stock, bring to the boil, then reduce the heat and simmer for 15 minutes, or until the squash is soft. Remove from the heat and leave to cool for 10 minutes. Using a blender or food processor, purée until completely smooth, adding salt and pepper to taste.

3. Ladle the soup into bowls, drizzle over a little extra-virgin olive oil, and top with the vegetable crisps and chives. Serve immediately. Alternatively, leave the soup to cool and then store in the fridge for up to three days. Reheat and garnish just before serving.

Tip
You can also make this with the same quantity of peeled sweet potato, or with any other variety of squash you come across.

SALADS & SIDES

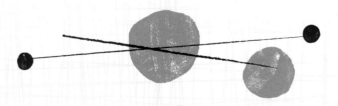

FIG, ROCKET & PECAN SALAD

Figs not only look beautiful in this salad, they also provide a gentle sweetness that pairs well with the mustardy kick of the rocket leaves and the crunchy pecan nuts.

Serves 4, as a side
Prep time: 5 minutes
Cook time: 5 minutes
VEGETARIAN

100g (4oz) pecan halves
4 fresh figs
200g (7oz) rocket
small handful of basil leaves
1 ball of buffalo mozzarella,
    torn into chunks
½ apple, cored and thinly sliced
3 tbsp extra-virgin olive oil
2 tbsp balsamic vinegar
1 tsp runny honey
sea salt and black pepper

1. Preheat the oven to 200°c/180°c fan/gas 6.

2. Roast the pecans on a baking sheet in the oven for 5 minutes, until a shade darker and aromatic.

3. Meanwhile, cut a cross into the top of each fig, then squeeze the bottom so the inner flesh opens out.

4. Toss the rocket and basil leaves with the mozzarella and sliced apple. Arrange on a plate and top with the figs and pecan nuts.

5. In a bowl, combine the oil, vinegar and honey and season to taste with salt and pepper. Drizzle over the salad and serve immediately.

WARM GOATS' CHEESE & ROASTED RED PEPPER SALAD

Using roasted red peppers from a jar (available in most supermarkets) means this salad comes together in record time. Cooking the courgette and chickpeas over a high heat gives a lovely smoky flavour.

Serves 4, as a light lunch
Prep time: 5 minutes
Cook time: 15 minutes
VEGETARIAN

60g (2½oz) walnuts
3 tbsp extra-virgin olive oil
1 courgette, roughly chopped
1 × 400g tin chickpeas, drained
    and rinsed
3 garlic cloves, crushed
300g (10½oz) roasted red peppers
    (from a jar), drained and
    thickly sliced
200g (7oz) goats' cheese log
    or round, thickly sliced
150g (5oz) mixed salad leaves
small handful of basil leaves
1 tbsp balsamic vinegar
sea salt and black pepper

1. Preheat the oven to 200°C/180°C fan/gas 6.

2. Roast the walnuts on a baking sheet in the oven for 4–5 minutes, until golden. Remove and set aside.

3. Heat one tablespoon of the oil in a pan over a high heat. Add the courgette and chickpeas and fry for 5–6 minutes until golden. Add the garlic and red pepper and stir-fry for a minute or two, until the garlic is aromatic and the red pepper is warmed through. Season well with salt and pepper and transfer to a bowl.

4. Wipe out the pan, add the goats' cheese slices and fry over a high heat for 30 seconds on each side until beginning to soften and melt.

5. Divide the mixed leaves and basil between four plates, top with the fried vegetables and chickpeas, goats' cheese slices and roasted walnuts and drizzle over the balsamic vinegar and the remaining olive oil. Serve immediately.

TORN CHICKEN & TOASTED BREAD SALAD

This is a gorgeous way to use up leftover roast chicken. It is also a good make-ahead salad, but don't add the dressing until just before serving.

Serves 4, as a light lunch
Prep time: 15 minutes

½ red onion, halved and
    very thinly sliced
1 red pepper, de-seeded and
    thinly sliced
1 green pepper, de-seeded
    and thinly sliced
1 cucumber, halved lengthways
    and thinly sliced
large handful of mint leaves,
    roughly chopped
large handful of flat-leaf parsley
    leaves, roughly chopped
2 thick slices of sourdough or
    rustic bread
600g (1lb 5oz) cooked chicken
grated zest and juice of 1 lemon
1 tsp runny honey
1 tsp wholegrain mustard
2 garlic cloves, crushed
5 tbsp extra-virgin olive oil
sea salt and black pepper

1. In a large bowl, combine the red onion, peppers, cucumber, mint and parsley.

2. Lightly toast the bread until golden and crisp, then tear into bite-sized chunks. Tear the chicken into rough strips, discarding any bones. Add the toasted bread and the chicken to the bowl of vegetables.

3. In a small bowl, whisk together the lemon zest and juice, honey, mustard, garlic and olive oil. Season to taste with salt and pepper and pour over the salad. Toss everything together until fully coated in the dressing. Serve immediately on a large platter.

Tip
If you want to make this from scratch, fry some chicken breasts or thighs until cooked through, then leave to rest for half an hour before you tear into strips.

SMOKED MACKEREL SALAD
WITH BEETROOT & HORSERADISH

This is quite a filling salad, and would make a perfect lunch,
or a starter before a light main course.

Serves 4, as a light lunch or starter
Prep time: 10 minutes
Cook time: 15–20 minutes

400g (14oz) new potatoes
   (no need to peel)
300g (10½oz) smoked mackerel
   fillets
250g (9oz) cooked beetroot (not in
   vinegar), cut into small wedges
150g (5oz) watercress and rocket
1 red pepper, de-seeded and
   roughly chopped
2 spring onions, thinly sliced
3 tbsp crème fraîche or
   natural yoghurt
2 tbsp extra-virgin olive oil
1–2 tbsp creamed horseradish
   (from a jar), to taste
sea salt and black pepper

1. Boil the potatoes in salted water for 15–20 minutes,
depending on their size, until a small sharp knife glides into
the centre of a potato without resistance. Drain the potatoes
and cut in half.

2. Meanwhile, break the mackerel into bite-sized pieces.
You can remove the skin first if you wish. Combine with the
beetroot, watercress and rocket, red pepper, spring onions
and halved potatoes. Season with salt and pepper and arrange
on a serving platter.

3. Combine the crème fraîche or yoghurt, olive oil and
horseradish. Season to taste with a little salt and pepper,
then dollop on top of the salad. Serve immediately.

CRAB, APPLE & SHAVED BRUSSELS SPROUT SALAD

If the idea of sprouts in anything other than Christmas dinner sends you running for the hills, you can of course use kale, cabbage or other salad leaves instead, but do try the sprouts – they are delicious with the sweet apple and mellow crab meat in this elegant starter.

Serves 4, as a light lunch or starter
Prep time: 25 minutes
Cook time: 5 minutes

25g (1oz) whole almonds, halved
3 tbsp natural Greek-style yoghurt
   or crème fraîche
1 lemon: grated zest and 2 tbsp juice
2 tsp wholegrain mustard
3 tbsp extra-virgin olive oil,
   plus extra to drizzle
300g (10½oz) fresh white and brown
   crab meat, picked through for
   pieces of shell
150g (5oz) Brussels sprouts,
   very finely sliced
2 spring onions, thinly sliced
1 apple, such as Cox's,
   cored and thinly sliced
1 fresh red chilli, de-seeded and
   thinly sliced
small handful of coriander leaves
75g (3oz) rocket and mixed
   salad leaves
sea salt and black pepper
1 lemon, cut into wedges,
   to serve (optional)

1. Preheat the oven to 200°C/180°C fan/gas 6.

2. Roast the almonds on a baking sheet in the oven for 5 minutes, until a shade darker and aromatic.

3. In a bowl, combine the yoghurt or crème fraîche with the lemon zest, juice, mustard and olive oil. Season to taste with salt and pepper.

4. Squeeze any excess liquid out of the picked crab. In a large mixing bowl, toss the crab with the Brussels sprouts and the dressing and most of the spring onions, apple, chilli and coriander.

5. Arrange the salad leaves and crab mixture on a plate. Scatter over the remaining spring onions, apple, chilli, coriander leaves and roasted almonds. Drizzle with a little extra-virgin olive oil. Serve with lemon wedges, if you like.

CHARRED BROCCOLI, CHESTNUTS & PANCETTA

This delicious side dish comes together in minutes, making it a great accompaniment to roasts. Whole cooked chestnuts in pouches or tins are easy to find in supermarkets, and they add a lovely texture and earthy flavour.

Serves 4, as a side
Prep time: 5 minutes
Cook time: 10 minutes

150g (5oz) thinly sliced pancetta
    (smoked or unsmoked),
    cut into small pieces
300g (10½oz) tenderstem broccoli,
    cut in half widthways if the
    stems are long
150g (5oz) cooked chestnuts, halved
2 tbsp olive oil
a handful of flat-leaf parsley leaves,
    chopped
sea salt and black pepper

1. Put the pancetta into a large non-stick pan and place over a high heat. Fry for 3–4 minutes until browned and crisp. Transfer the pancetta to a bowl, keeping the fat that has rendered from the pancetta in the pan.

2. Add the broccoli and chestnuts to the pan with the olive oil and stir-fry over a medium–high heat for 4–5 minutes until the broccoli is slightly charred and cooked through, but still retaining a bite.

3. Return the pancetta to the pan, taste, and season with pepper and a little salt, bearing in mind the pancetta is already salty. Stir through the parsley and serve immediately.

BRAISED CABBAGE WITH FRIED BREAD, BACON & PARSLEY

If you are of the opinion that cabbage is bland and unexciting, try this dish. First fried and then simmered in stock, the cabbage is transformed into something truly delicious.

Serves 4, as a side
Prep time: 5 minutes
Cook time: 30 minutes

3 tbsp salted butter
1 pointed spring cabbage,
    outer leaves removed,
    halved lengthways
200ml (7fl oz) chicken or
    vegetable stock
1 tbsp olive oil
2 slices of sourdough or rustic bread,
    chopped into small pieces
4 rashers smoked or unsmoked
    rindless bacon, cut into
    small pieces
small handful of flat-leaf parsley
    leaves, roughly chopped
sea salt and black pepper

1. Heat the butter in a large pan (with a lid) over a medium heat. When the butter is sizzling, add the cabbage, cut side down. Fry for 4–6 minutes until lightly golden.

2. Pour in the stock and immediately cover with the lid. Reduce the heat to medium–low and cook for 18–22 minutes, depending on the size of the cabbage, until tender and a sharp knife glides into the centre without resistance. Remove to a plate, season with salt and pepper and keep warm. The stock can be discarded or saved for something else.

3. Wipe the pan and return to the heat. Add the oil, bread and bacon. Fry over a medium–high heat until the bread and bacon are deep golden and crisp. Remove from the heat and stir through the parsley.

4. Serve the cabbage immediately, with the fried bread, bacon and parsley scattered over.

NEW POTATOES
WITH DILL & PARSLEY

Waxy and firm new potatoes, boiled and topped with salted butter and fragrant herbs, are always a delicious accompaniment to meat or fish.

Serves 6, as a side
Prep time: 5 minutes
Cook time: 15–20 minutes
VEGETARIAN

1kg (2lb 3oz) new potatoes
(no need to peel)
3 tbsp salted butter
small handful of dill fronds,
roughly chopped
small handful of flat-leaf parsley
leaves, roughly chopped
sea salt and black pepper

1. Bring a large pan of salted water to the boil. Add the potatoes and cook for 15–20 minutes until a sharp knife glides into the centre of a potato without resistance.

2. Drain the potatoes, return to the pan and toss with the butter and most of the herbs. Transfer to a serving dish, top with the remaining herbs and season with salt and pepper. Serve immediately.

Tip
Feel free to swap the dill and parsley for other herbs, if you prefer. Samphire and wild garlic are also delicious when in season.

CUMIN & CLEMENTINE
SPICED CARROTS

Cumin and clementine juice are a perfect combination and make these baby carrots irresistible. Photographed overleaf.

Serves 3–4, as a side
Prep time: 10 minutes
Cook time: 15–20 minutes
VEGETARIAN

250g (9oz) baby carrots,
    any combination of colours,
    peeled and tops trimmed
2 tbsp sunflower oil
1 tsp cumin seeds
1 garlic clove, crushed
1 tbsp runny honey
juice of ½ clementine
1 tsp fresh thyme leaves
sea salt and black pepper

1. Bring a large pan of salted water to the boil and put the carrots in to cook for 10–15 minutes until just tender, then drain.

2. Heat the oil in a large pan over a medium–high heat. Add the carrots, cumin seeds, garlic, honey and clementine juice. Season well with salt and pepper and cook for 3–5 minutes until all the liquid has evaporated. Remove from the heat and sprinkle over the thyme. Serve immediately.

Best of
HOME
COOK

GOLDEN BOMBAY POTATOES

A simple potato side dish gets a lift with warming spices. Perfect served with the Spiced Roast Chicken (page 138) or with the Pan-fried Spicy Mackerel (page 207). Photographed overleaf.

Serves 6–8, as a side
Prep time: 5 minutes
Cook time: 1 hour
VEGETARIAN

½ tsp ground turmeric
2kg (4lb 6oz) floury potatoes
    (such as Maris Piper), unpeeled
6 garlic cloves, unpeeled
40g (1½oz) unsalted butter
5 tbsp sunflower oil
pinch of cumin seeds
½ tsp ground cumin
sea salt

1. Preheat the oven to 190°C/170°C fan/gas 5.

2. Bring a very large pan of water to the boil and add the turmeric and one teaspoon of salt. Lightly score the potatoes on each side in a criss-cross pattern, add to the pan and parboil for 10 minutes, then drain.

3. Transfer the potatoes to a roasting tin with the whole garlic cloves. Heat the butter and oil in a pan with the cumin seeds, ground cumin and a large pinch of salt, just until the butter has melted. Pour over the potatoes and turn to coat.

4. Roast for 30 minutes, then increase the heat to 220°C/ 200°C fan/gas 7 and cook for a further 20–25 minutes until tender. Serve hot. The roasted garlic cloves can be squeezed from their skins and enjoyed alongside.

Best of
HOME
COOK

SMASHED COURGETTES WITH TOMATO & CUMIN

If you are ever in need of a last-minute vegetable side dish, this is the one to make. Full of flavour, it comes together in no time at all. Smashing the courgette may seem a little unusual, but it provides a lovely rough edge and texture that looks great once plated up.

Serves 4, as a side
Prep time: 5 minutes
Cook time: 12 minutes
VEGETARIAN
VEGAN

3 courgettes
4 tbsp olive oil
250g (9oz) cherry tomatoes, halved
4 garlic cloves, crushed
2 tsp cumin seeds
dried chilli flakes (optional)
sea salt and black pepper

1. Gently bash each courgette with a rolling pin or a tin of beans, until it cracks open and breaks into rough shapes. Alternatively, cut the courgettes into rough, uneven shapes.

2. Heat the olive oil in a large pan over a high heat. Add the smashed courgettes and stir-fry for 5 minutes, until golden. Add the tomatoes and fry for another 4–5 minutes. Turn down the heat, add the garlic and cumin seeds and fry for another 1–2 minutes, until aromatic. Season well with salt and pepper.

3. Serve immediately with the chilli flakes scattered over, if you like.

ROSEMARY YORKSHIRE PUDDINGS

Chopped rosemary adds a gentle perfume to classic Yorkshire puddings, making them a perfect match for roast lamb.

Makes 12 Yorkshire puddings
Prep time: 10 minutes,
    plus 1 hour chilling
Cook time: 18–22 minutes
VEGETARIAN

150g (5oz) plain flour, sifted
3 eggs
200ml (7fl oz) whole milk
1 tsp fine sea salt
3 rosemary sprigs, leaves removed
    and very finely chopped
4 tbsp vegetable oil

1. Put the flour, eggs and half the milk into a bowl and whisk to combine. Slowly whisk in the remaining milk with the salt and chopped rosemary until the batter is completely smooth. Cover and chill in the refrigerator for 1 hour.

2. When ready to cook, preheat the oven to 220°C/200°C fan/ gas 7. Divide the oil evenly between the cups of a 12-hole muffin tin and put the tin into the oven to heat up for 10 minutes.

3. Carefully and evenly ladle the batter into the cups of hot oil and cook for 18–22 minutes or until deep golden brown and well risen. Serve immediately.

Best of
HOME
COOK

VEGETABLE MAINS

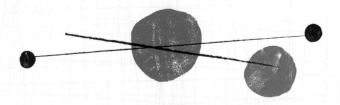

SWEET POTATO, PESTO & GOATS' CHEESE FRITTATA

A frittata is a great make-ahead meal, either for dinner or for a packed lunch. You can use other vegetables, depending on what you have available, but ensure they are cooked before you mix them with the egg mixture.

Serves 6–8
Prep time: 10 minutes
Cook time: 1 hour 10 minutes
VEGETARIAN

300g (10½oz) sweet potatoes,
    cut into bite-sized chunks
    (no need to peel)
3 tbsp olive oil
1 red onion, sliced
200g (7oz) cherry tomatoes
250g (9oz) fresh spinach, washed
12 eggs
3 tbsp pesto (of your choice),
    plus extra to serve
100g (4oz) goats' cheese, crumbled
sea salt and black pepper
mixed salad leaves, to serve

1. Preheat the oven to 200°C/180°C fan/gas 6.

2. Put the sweet potato and two tablespoons of the olive oil into a roasting tin, toss and season well with salt and pepper. Roast for 15 minutes. Toss the red onion and tomatoes in the remaining olive oil, season with salt and pepper and add to the tin. Roast for another 10 minutes, then remove and set aside.

3. Meanwhile, put the spinach in a large pan and place over a high heat. Turn the spinach from time to time as it wilts down, then drain in a sieve, pressing out any excess water. Season with a little salt.

4. Crack the eggs into a large bowl, whisk together with the pesto and season with three-quarters of a teaspoon of salt and a large pinch of pepper. Pour the egg mixture into a 25cm (10in) ovenproof frying pan or quiche dish. Add the sweet potato, onion, tomatoes and spinach so you can see their colours peeping out above the egg mixture. Scatter over the goats' cheese and season again with a little salt and pepper.

5. Bake for 35–40 minutes, until the frittata has puffed up and the top is just firm to the touch. If it is still uncooked in the centre, cover with foil to prevent burning and cook for another 5–10 minutes until just firm.

6. Let the frittata cool a little, then serve in wedges with a drizzle of pesto and a mixed leaf salad.

MUSHROOM, TOMATO & MOZZARELLA STUFFED PEPPERS

Cannellini beans provide a dense and creamy base for the mushroom, tomato and mozzarella filling. They do need quite a bit of seasoning, so remember to taste the mixture before you spoon it into the halved peppers.

Serves 4
Prep time: 15 minutes
Cook time: 35 minutes
VEGETARIAN

4 red peppers, halved and de-seeded
3 tbsp olive oil
300g (10½oz) fresh shiitake mushrooms, thinly sliced
1 onion, finely chopped
3 garlic cloves, crushed
1 × 400g tin cannellini beans, drained, rinsed and lightly mashed
200g (7oz) cherry tomatoes, roughly chopped
1 ball of buffalo mozzarella, torn into bite-sized pieces
2 tsp fresh lemon juice
large handful of basil leaves, finely chopped
1 tbsp fresh thyme leaves
sea salt and black pepper
green salad, to serve

1. Preheat the oven to 200°C/180°C fan/gas 6. Line a baking sheet (or baking tin) with baking parchment.

2. Put the peppers onto the lined baking sheet and coat with one tablespoon of the olive oil. Season well with salt and pepper and bake for 20 minutes, or until beginning to soften but still holding their shape.

3. Meanwhile, heat the remaining oil in a pan over a medium–high heat. Add the mushrooms and onion and fry for 10 minutes until the onion is translucent and the mushrooms are golden. Add the garlic and fry for another 2 minutes until aromatic. Add the cannellini beans to the pan, together with the tomatoes, mozzarella, lemon juice, basil and thyme. Mix together and season to taste with salt and pepper, then remove from the heat.

4. Remove the peppers from the oven and divide the mixture between them, then return to the oven for 15 minutes.

5. Serve immediately, with a green salad.

Tip
If fresh shiitake mushrooms are not available, you could replace them with chestnut mushrooms.

SWEET POTATO, RED LENTIL & COCONUT CURRY

This warming curry is brought together by the red lentils, which become thick and creamy as they cook. This can be made in advance and frozen in batches if you wish.

Serves 4
Prep time: 10 minutes
Cook time: 50 minutes
VEGETARIAN
VEGAN – see tip

2 tbsp olive oil
1 red onion, roughly chopped
5 garlic cloves, crushed
½ tsp dried chilli flakes
2 tsp garam masala
1 tsp ground coriander
1 tsp ground cumin
1 tsp ground turmeric
2 sweet potatoes, chopped into
    bite-sized pieces (no need to peel)
150g (5oz) red lentils
400ml (14fl oz) coconut milk
500ml (17fl oz) vegetable stock
150g (5oz) fresh spinach, washed
2 tbsp fresh lemon juice
sea salt and black pepper

To serve
cooked rice
natural yoghurt
large handful of coriander leaves

1. Heat the oil in a large deep pan over a medium heat. Add the onion and sauté for 5 minutes until beginning to soften. Add the garlic, chilli flakes, garam masala, ground coriander, cumin and turmeric. Fry for 3–4 minutes, stirring now and again, until aromatic.

2. Add the sweet potatoes, lentils, coconut milk and stock and bring to the boil. Reduce the heat and simmer for 30–35 minutes, stirring frequently to prevent the lentils from sticking, until the sweet potatoes and lentils are cooked through.

3. Add the spinach to the pan and cook for 5 minutes until wilted down. Stir in the lemon juice and season to taste with up to a teaspoon of salt and a grinding of black pepper.

4. Serve with rice, a dollop of yoghurt and coriander leaves scattered over.

Tip
This is vegan, apart from the yoghurt that is served with it; you can use a dairy-free alternative to yoghurt, if you prefer.

THAI AUBERGINE CURRY

Aubergine is a wonderful vegetable for taking on flavour, which certainly isn't lacking in this addictive Thai curry. The flavours get even better overnight, so this is a great make-ahead dish.

Best of
HOME
COOK

Serves 4
Prep time: 15 minutes
Cook time: 45 minutes
VEGETARIAN – see tip

5 tbsp sunflower oil
2 aubergines, cut into batons 2cm (¾in) thick
1 onion, peeled and quartered
4 garlic cloves, peeled
3cm (about 1in) piece of fresh root ginger, peeled
2 sticks of lemongrass, tough outer leaves removed, roughly chopped
5 cardamom pods
1 tbsp cumin seeds
1 tbsp coriander seeds
1 tsp ground turmeric
¼ tsp ground nutmeg
1 tbsp caster sugar
3 tbsp peanut or cashew butter
400ml (14fl oz) coconut milk
250ml (9fl oz) chicken stock
1 fresh red chilli, de-seeded and sliced
150g (5oz) fresh spinach, washed
2 tbsp fish sauce
1 tbsp fresh lemon juice
small handful of Thai basil leaves
sea salt
cooked rice, to serve

1. In a bowl, combine three tablespoons of the oil, the aubergine batons and half a teaspoon of salt. Fry in a large pan over a high heat for 8–10 minutes, stirring frequently, until beginning to char. Don't worry if the aubergine is not completely cooked through, as it will be added to the curry later. Set aside.

2. Put the onion, garlic, ginger and lemongrass into a food processor and blitz until finely ground.

3. Bash open the cardamom pods, discard the skins and put the seeds into a dry pan, together with the cumin and coriander seeds. Place over a medium heat and cook for 2–3 minutes until aromatic. Transfer to a mortar or spice grinder and grind to a powder. Tip the powder into a bowl and combine with the onion and garlic mixture, turmeric, nutmeg, sugar and peanut or cashew butter.

4. Heat the remaining two tablespoons of oil in a wok or large deep pan over a medium heat. Add the curry paste mixture and fry, stirring now and again, for 3–5 minutes until cooked through and fragrant. Add the coconut milk and stock and bring to the boil. Reduce the heat to a simmer, add the aubergines and most of the chilli and cook for 15–20 minutes until slightly reduced and the aubergine is soft. Stir in the spinach until wilted down.

5. Add the fish sauce and lemon juice, taste and adjust the seasoning if necessary. Scatter over the Thai basil leaves and remaining chilli and serve with rice.

Tip
If you are vegetarian, replace the chicken stock with vegetable stock and replace the fish sauce with soy sauce.

CHICKPEA, TOMATO & CHARD STEW

This is an easy stew that can be made in double or triple quantities, portioned up and frozen, ready for the week ahead. Chickpeas in tins work well here, but chickpeas in glass jars often have a better texture, so stock up on them if you ever come across them (see tip).

Serves 4
Prep time: 15 minutes
Cook time: 50 minutes
VEGETARIAN– see tip
VEGAN– see tip

3 tbsp extra-virgin olive oil, plus
    extra to drizzle
1 onion, chopped
1 tsp dried chilli flakes
1 tsp ground cumin
6 garlic cloves, crushed
4 rosemary sprigs, leaves removed
2 × 400g tins chickpeas, drained
    and rinsed
2 × 400g tins peeled plum tomatoes
300ml (½ pint) chicken or
    vegetable stock
275g (10oz) Swiss chard, chopped
    into bite-sized pieces
75g (3oz) Parmesan, grated
sea salt and black pepper

1. Heat the oil in a large deep pan over a medium heat. Add the onion, most of the chilli flakes, the cumin, garlic and rosemary leaves and gently cook for 10 minutes until the onion is soft and translucent. Stir frequently and reduce the heat if the garlic is beginning to catch.

2. Using a potato masher, roughly mash half the chickpeas until just broken down. Add them to the pan with the tomatoes and stock. Bring to the boil, then reduce the heat and simmer for 25 minutes. Season with a pinch of salt and pepper.

3. Add the chard to the pan and simmer for 5 minutes until the stalks are becoming tender. Add most of the grated Parmesan, mix together and simmer for another 5 minutes. Taste and adjust the seasoning if necessary with more salt and pepper.

4. Serve in bowls with the remaining Parmesan and chilli scattered over and a drizzle of olive oil.

Tips
If you are using dried chickpeas that you have soaked and cooked, or chickpeas from a jar, you will need about 500g (1lb 2oz) (drained weight).

If you are vegetarian or vegan, use vegetable stock.

If you are vegetarian, look for vegetarian Italian-style hard cheese, as Parmesan is made with animal rennet.

For a vegan dish, swap the Parmesan for a little miso and nutritional yeast.

BUBBLE & SQUEAK

Traditionally, bubble and squeak is a simple combination of leftover mashed potato and cabbage. The key is to get the patties golden and crispy on the outside, the perfect foil for the soft, comforting mash on the inside. Serve with bacon and eggs to take them to another level.

Serves 4
Prep time: 10 minutes
Cook time: 25 minutes
VEGETARIAN – see tip
VEGAN – see tip

4 tbsp olive oil
250g (9oz) cabbage, Brussels sprouts or kale, finely shredded
1 onion, very finely chopped
1 garlic clove, crushed
500g (1lb 2oz) mashed potato (see tip if using boiled)
7 tbsp plain flour
2 tbsp salted butter
8 rashers bacon (optional)
4 eggs (optional)
sea salt and black pepper

1. Heat two tablespoons of the olive oil in a frying pan over a medium–high heat. Add the shredded cabbage, sprouts or kale and the onion and cook for 6–8 minutes, tossing now and again, until the leaves have wilted down and the onion is translucent. Add the garlic and fry for another 2 minutes until aromatic. Transfer to a large bowl.

2. Add the mashed potato and flour to the bowl of cooked cabbage. Season to taste with salt and pepper and mix everything together until thoroughly combined. Shape the mixture into eight patties.

3. Put the butter and the remaining two tablespoons of oil into the pan and set over a medium heat. Cook the potato cakes in batches, for 3–4 minutes on each side, until golden and crisp. Handle them gently as they are quite fragile. Remove and keep warm.

4. Fry up the bacon and eggs to your liking and serve immediately with the bubble and squeak.

Tips
If you are vegetarian or vegan, use oil instead of butter and omit the eggs and bacon, serving the potato cakes as they are or with a salad.

If you don't have leftover mashed potato, peel and boil 500g (1lb 2oz) floury potatoes (such as King Edward), then mash them with four tablespoons of salted butter before you continue. Leftover roast potatoes are not ideal for this recipe.

SQUASH WITH CANNELLINI BEANS, TOMATOES, FETA & BASIL

Vibrantly coloured roasted autumn squash is an ideal centrepiece for a vegetarian or vegan meal. To make a vegan dish, leave out the feta and replace with a handful of mixed pitted olives.

Serves 4
Prep time: 15 minutes
Cook time: 45–55 minutes
VEGETARIAN
VEGAN – see note in introduction

2 large butternut or onion squash
6 tbsp olive oil
1 × 400g tin cannellini beans, drained and rinsed
200g (7oz) cherry tomatoes, halved
2 garlic cloves, crushed
150g (5oz) feta, crumbled
small handful of basil leaves
sea salt and black pepper

1. Preheat the oven to 180°c/160°c fan/gas 4.

2. Cut both squash in half lengthways, scoop out the seeds and cut lengthways again, to make eight pieces in total. The skin of onion squash is tender and delicious to eat, so there is no need to peel. The skin of butternut squash is a little tougher: you can eat it, but you may prefer to peel it.

3. Transfer the squash to a large roasting tin and coat with four tablespoons of the olive oil. Season well with salt and pepper and roast for 45–55 minutes, depending on the size of the squash pieces, until they are golden and a sharp knife glides easily into the flesh.

4. Meanwhile, put the cannellini beans and tomatoes into a bowl. Add the remaining two tablespoons of olive oil and the garlic, season with salt and pepper and mix together. After the squash has been in the oven for 35–40 minutes, add the beans and tomatoes to the roasting tin to warm through.

5. Once the squash is cooked, remove from the oven and divide between four plates, with a serving of the bean and tomato mixture. Scatter over the crumbled feta and the basil leaves and serve immediately.

PORTOBELLO MUSHROOMS, SPINACH & SPICED HUMMUS

Garlic mushrooms are perfect with gently spiced hummus and spinach. This makes an excellent vegetarian or vegan main course.

Serves 4
Prep time: 10 minutes
Cook time: 15 minutes
VEGETARIAN
VEGAN

8 Portobello mushrooms
1 garlic clove, crushed
4 tbsp extra-virgin olive oil
250g (9oz) spinach, washed
1 spring onion, sliced
½ tsp dried chilli flakes (optional)
sea salt and black pepper

For the spiced hummus
2 × 400g tins chickpeas, drained
    and rinsed
100g (4oz) tahini
juice of 1 lemon, or more to taste
1 tbsp mild curry powder
2 garlic cloves, crushed
2 tbsp extra-virgin olive oil,
    or more to taste
4 tbsp water

1. Trim the stalks of the mushrooms so they can be laid flat in a pan, then put them in a bowl and add the garlic and olive oil.

2. For the hummus, put the chickpeas, tahini, lemon juice, curry powder, garlic, olive oil and water into a food processor and purée until smooth and creamy. Season to taste with salt and add a little more olive oil, water and lemon juice, if needed.

3. Place a griddle pan or heavy-based frying pan over a medium heat. Season the mushrooms with salt and pepper and cook on the hot pan for 5–6 minutes on each side, until cooked through and slightly charred.

4. Meanwhile, put the spinach in a large pan and place over a high heat. Turn the spinach from time to time for 2–3 minutes, until it has wilted down completely. Drain in a sieve and season with salt and pepper.

5. To serve, divide the hummus between four plates and place the mushrooms on top with the spinach. Scatter over the spring onion and chilli flakes, if using. Serve immediately.

RAINBOW VEGETABLE BAKE WITH MOZZARELLA & ROSEMARY

A comforting dish, full of the flavours of the Mediterranean, this can also be made ahead of time, left to cool, and reheated just before serving.

Serves 6
Prep time: 10 minutes
Cook time: 45–55 minutes
VEGETARIAN – see tip

1 × 400g tin chopped tomatoes
1 tsp ground cumin
¼ tsp smoked paprika (optional)
1 large sweet potato, very thinly sliced lengthways (no need to peel)
250g (9oz) cooked beetroot (not in vinegar), very thinly sliced
150g (5oz) roasted red peppers (from a jar), drained and sliced
2 courgettes, very thinly sliced lengthways
2 balls of buffalo mozzarella, drained and thinly sliced
olive oil, for greasing and to drizzle
Parmesan, to grate on top
2 tbsp finely chopped rosemary leaves
sea salt and black pepper
green salad, to serve

1. Preheat the oven to 200°c/180°c fan/gas 6. Grease a 23 × 18cm (9 × 7in) baking dish with olive oil.

2. Put the tomatoes into a pan and bring to the boil. Remove from the heat and season with the cumin, paprika (if using) and salt and pepper to taste. Set aside.

3. Arrange the slices of sweet potato, beetroot, red pepper, courgette and mozzarella in layers in the baking dish, seasoning each layer with a pinch of salt and pepper, a drizzle of olive oil and a few spoons of the seasoned tomatoes. Keep layering until you have used up all of the vegetables, mozzarella and tomatoes. Grate some Parmesan over the top and sprinkle over the rosemary leaves.

4. Bake for 45–55 minutes until the top is bubbling and golden and a sharp knife glides into the centre without resistance. If the top is browning too quickly, loosely cover with foil. Serve immediately, with a green salad.

Tip
If you are vegetarian, look for vegetarian Italian-style hard cheese, as Parmesan is made with animal rennet. Alternatively, use extra mozzarella.

JERUSALEM ARTICHOKE & CELERIAC GRATIN

The subtle earthy flavours of celeriac and Jerusalem artichoke are a perfect match in this simple gratin.

Best of
HOME
COOK

Serves 4
Prep time: 10 minutes
Cook time: 1 hour
VEGETARIAN – see tip

100ml (3½fl oz) double cream
100ml (3½fl oz) milk
2 bay leaves
¼ tsp ground nutmeg
1 garlic clove, crushed
250g (9oz) celeriac, peeled
250g (9oz) Jerusalem artichokes,
    scrubbed if necessary
50g (2oz) fresh breadcrumbs
2 tbsp fresh thyme leaves
40g (1½oz) Parmesan, grated
sea salt and black pepper

1. Preheat the oven to 200°C/180°C fan/gas 6.

2. Put the cream, milk, bay leaves, nutmeg and garlic into a pan and bring to the boil, then reduce the heat to low and simmer for 2 minutes. Remove from the heat and leave to infuse for 5 minutes. Remove the bay leaves.

3. Thinly slice the celeriac and Jerusalem artichokes and set to one side.

4. In a bowl, combine the breadcrumbs, thyme and Parmesan. Layer the sliced vegetables in a baking dish, seasoning each layer with salt and pepper as you go. Pour over the cream mixture, then scatter the breadcrumb mixture evenly over the top. Cover tightly with foil and bake for 30 minutes.

5. Remove the foil and bake for a further 20 minutes until cooked through and golden on top. Serve immediately.

Tip
If you are vegetarian, look for vegetarian Italian-style hard cheese, as Parmesan is made with animal rennet.

CAULIFLOWER CHEESE

A little mustard brings out the flavour of the cheese in this classic and comforting dish.

Best of
HOME
COOK

Serves 4
Prep time: 10 minutes
Cook time: 40 minutes
VEGETARIAN

1 large cauliflower, about 900g (2lb),
    leaves removed
4 tbsp olive oil
60g (2½oz) unsalted butter
50g (2oz) plain flour
450ml (¾ pint) whole milk
85g (3½oz) Lancashire cheese,
    crumbled
1 tbsp Dijon mustard
40g (1½oz) Cheddar, grated
small handful of flat-leaf parsley
    leaves, chopped
sea salt and black pepper

1. Preheat the oven to 220°C/200°C fan/gas 7.

2. Break the cauliflower into medium-sized florets and put them on a large baking sheet. Add the olive oil and toss together; season well with salt and pepper. Roast for 15 minutes until golden, then remove and set aside. Leave the oven on.

3. Melt the butter in a pan over a medium–low heat, add the flour, stir to combine and then cook, stirring all the time, for 2 minutes. Add the milk a little at a time, stirring constantly until smooth. Bring to the boil, then reduce the heat and simmer for 5 minutes, stirring frequently, until thickened. Season to taste with salt and pepper.

4. Remove the sauce from the heat and stir in the Lancashire cheese and mustard. Add the cauliflower and stir to combine. Transfer to a baking dish, scatter over the Cheddar and season with a little pepper.

5. Bake for about 15 minutes, until the sauce is bubbling and the cheese on top is golden brown. Scatter over the parsley and serve immediately.

PASTA, RICE & GRAINS

SPINACH & RICOTTA RAVIOLI WITH SAGE BUTTER

Making your own pasta does take a bit of time, but if you have a pasta machine the process is reasonably straightforward and the rewards are great, as home-made ravioli truly is a thing of beauty.

Serves 4–6
Prep time: 1 hour 10 minutes,
    plus 45 minutes chilling
Cook time: 15 minutes
VEGETARIAN – see tip overleaf

360g (12½oz) 00 flour, or strong
    white bread flour, plus extra
    for dusting
4 eggs
200g (7oz) fresh spinach, washed
    and drained
200g (7oz) ricotta
40g (1½oz) Parmesan, finely grated,
    plus extra to serve
grated zest of 1 lemon
20g (¾oz) fresh sage leaves,
    stalks discarded
1 garlic clove, crushed
100g (4oz) unsalted butter
sea salt and black pepper

1. Put the flour, eggs and a large pinch of salt into the bowl of a stand mixer fitted with a dough hook and mix gently until it comes together. It may seem very dry at first, but it will gradually form a dough. If, after a minute or so, it still seems crumbly, add in one to two teaspoons of water, kneading after each addition. Continue to knead for 6–8 minutes until the dough is smooth and stretchy, and springs back when you press your finger into it. Divide the dough into four equal pieces, wrap tightly in clingfilm and refrigerate for at least 45 minutes.

2. Meanwhile, put the spinach into a large dry frying pan and place over a high heat. Cook the spinach, turning frequently, for 3–5 minutes until it has completely wilted down. Drain in a sieve, pressing out as much liquid as possible, then wrap in a clean tea towel and press out any remaining liquid, so the spinach is as dry as possible. Finely chop the spinach and transfer to a bowl, together with the ricotta, Parmesan and lemon zest. Season to taste with salt and plenty of black pepper and set to one side.

3. Put the sage, garlic and butter into a pan large enough to hold all the pasta once cooked. Place over a medium–low heat until the butter melts, simmer gently for 5 minutes, then remove from the heat and leave to infuse. Season with a pinch of salt and pepper.

4. Take one portion of dough from the fridge, remove the clingfilm and lightly dust the dough with flour. Flatten with a rolling pin to the width of your pasta machine. Feed the dough through on the widest setting, then fold each side of the dough to the centre, as if you were folding a letter to fit inside an envelope. Feed the dough through on the widest setting again. Adjust the

Recipe continues overleaf

rollers to the next setting and roll the dough through the pasta machine again. Continue to roll the dough through the machine, decreasing the thickness by one setting each time and dusting with a little more flour if it becomes sticky. Do not be tempted to skip settings on the pasta machine, otherwise the dough may tear.

5. Once you have rolled it through on the thinnest setting, cut the long sheet of pasta in half widthways. Lay one length on a floured work surface and set the other half to one side, covered with a clean damp tea towel.

6. Place teaspoonfuls of the ricotta mixture at even intervals along the middle of the pasta sheet, using no more than about a quarter of the mixture. You should be able to fit about nine teaspoons of filling along the sheet of pasta.

7. Using a pastry brush and water, dampen the pasta around the ricotta filling. Now take the other half sheet of pasta and carefully lay it over the ricotta, gently pressing down around the mounds of filling and pushing out any air pockets. Using a sharp knife, trim the pasta into evenly sized squares of ravioli, then lay them out on a tray, dust with a little flour and cover with clingfilm. Keep the trimmings for other pasta dishes, or to throw into a soup. Roll out and fill the remaining three pieces of pasta in the same way.

8. When ready to serve, bring a large pan of salted water to the boil and place the pan of sage butter over a low heat. Cook the ravioli (in batches if necessary) in the boiling water for about 3 minutes. Remove with a slotted spoon and add to the pan of sage butter. Gently stir to combine, then serve immediately with a little more Parmesan and black pepper.

Tip
If you are vegetarian, look for vegetarian Italian-style hard cheese, as Parmesan is made with animal rennet.

CREAMY SALMON, PRAWN & MUSSEL PASTA WITH SAMPHIRE

Samphire, a salty marsh grass, is delicious with fish and shellfish, its bright colour and fresh flavour providing a lovely contrast to the creamy pasta sauce. Cod can be used instead of the salmon.

Best of
HOME
COOK

Serves 4
Prep time: 15 minutes
Cook time: 45 minutes

3 tbsp olive oil
1 onion, finely chopped
3 garlic cloves, crushed
300ml (½ pint) Prosecco
200g (7oz) fresh mussels, cleaned
　(see tip opposite)
500ml (17fl oz) fresh fish stock
400g (14oz) salmon fillet, skinned
　and cut into bite-sized pieces
8 peeled raw tiger prawns
60g (2½oz) samphire
350g (12oz) linguine
50g (2oz) salted butter
150ml (¼ pint) double cream
100g (4oz) Wensleydale cheese
small handful flat-leaf parsley
　leaves, roughly chopped
small handful of chives,
　roughly chopped
1 tbsp fresh lemon juice
sea salt and black pepper

1. Heat the oil in a large heavy-based pan (with a lid) over a medium–low heat. Add the onion and garlic and sauté for 8–10 minutes until the onions are soft.

2. Add 75ml (2½fl oz) of the Prosecco and bring to the boil. Add the mussels, cover with the lid and cook for about 3 minutes until the shells have opened. Using a slotted spoon, transfer the mussels to a plate and discard any that have not opened up.

3. Pour the fish stock into the pan and bring to a simmer. Add the salmon and prawns and poach for 2 minutes, or until just cooked through. Using a slotted spoon, remove the fish and prawns and set to one side. Pour the remaining Prosecco into the pan and bring to the boil. Keep at a rolling boil for about 20 minutes until the liquid has reduced by half.

4. Meanwhile, bring a large pan of water to the boil and cook the samphire for 3 minutes. Using a slotted spoon, transfer to a bowl and combine with one tablespoon of the butter until melted.

5. Salt the boiling water, add the pasta and cook according to the packet instructions, then drain and return to the pan.

6. Once the sauce has reduced by half, lower the heat to a simmer, stir in the cream and the remaining butter and simmer for 8–10 minutes until thickened. Crumble in the cheese and stir to combine. Add the cooked fish and shellfish to the sauce and heat through; taste and adjust the seasoning, adding salt and pepper to taste. Combine the fish and sauce with the cooked pasta, parsley, chives and lemon juice. Serve immediately, with the samphire on top.

To clean the mussels, put them into a bowl of cold water, discarding any broken shells. Scrape off any large barnacles and pull away the hairy 'beards'. Discard any shells that remain open when tapped sharply against your work surface.

PASTA WITH CHANTERELLES, WALNUTS, LEMON & GARLIC

This easy recipe is made with ready-made pappardelle, which means you can enjoy the buttery, garlicky flavours of this comforting dish, with earthy chanterelle mushrooms and crunchy walnut pieces, without the added work of having to make your own pasta.

Serves 4
Prep time: 15 minutes
Cook time: 15 minutes
VEGETARIAN – see tip

450g (1lb) pappardelle or tagliatelle
4 tbsp extra-virgin olive oil, plus extra to drizzle
5 tbsp salted butter
200g (7oz) chanterelle mushrooms, sliced (see tip)
600g (1lb 5oz) mixed fresh mushrooms, thinly sliced
50 g (2oz) walnuts, finely chopped
4 garlic cloves, crushed
grated zest of 2 lemons
small handful of parsley leaves, roughly chopped
4 tbsp freshly grated Parmesan, plus extra to serve
sea salt and black pepper

1. Bring a large pan of salted water to the boil. Cook the pasta according to the packet instructions, then drain and return to the pan.

2. While the pasta is cooking, put the oil and half the butter into a large pan over a medium–high heat. Add all the mushrooms and walnuts and fry for 6–8 minutes, tossing now and again, until the mushrooms have released their liquid and become tender and golden.

3. Add the rest of the butter, the garlic and lemon zest to the pan. Fry for another 4–5 minutes until aromatic and the mushrooms and walnut pieces are deeply golden. Season well with salt and pepper.

4. Add the mushroom mixture to the cooked pasta, along with the parsley and Parmesan and gently combine, adding a little more olive oil. Taste and adjust the seasoning if necessary. Serve with extra Parmesan to scatter on top, if you like.

Tips
If you can't get hold of chanterelles (also known as girolles), shiitake or other wild mushrooms are a great alternative.

If you are vegetarian, look for vegetarian Italian-style hard cheese, as Parmesan is made with animal rennet.

BEETROOT GNOCCHI & SPINACH

Gnocchi are a tasty alternative to pasta. While they do take time to make, the process is reasonably simple. Here, the beetroot provides a lovely earthy flavour and a beautiful colour. If you are vegetarian, replace the Parmesan with vegetarian Italian-style hard cheese.

Serves 4
Prep time: 40 minutes, plus cooling
Cook time: 1 hour 20 minutes
VEGETARIAN – see note in
    introduction

500g (1lb 2oz) evenly sized floury
    potatoes (such as Maris Piper),
    unpeeled
120g (4½oz) cooked beetroot
    (not in vinegar), peeled
1 egg, beaten
200g (7oz) plain flour, plus extra
    for dusting
3 tbsp extra-virgin olive oil, plus
    extra to drizzle
200g (7oz) cherry tomatoes, halved
200g (7oz) fresh spinach, washed
    and drained
6 tbsp unsalted butter
5 garlic cloves, crushed
50g (2oz) Parmesan, grated,
    plus extra to serve
sea salt and black pepper

1. Preheat the oven to 200°C/180°C fan/gas 6. Prick the potatoes and bake for about an hour or until cooked through and tender. Remove and leave to cool for 10 minutes, then cut in half and scoop out as much of the flesh as possible. You should have about 275g (10oz). Mash the potato, then press it through a fine sieve to get it as smooth as possible.

2. Using a blender or food processor, purée 75g (3oz) of the beetroot until smooth, then press through a sieve. Dice the remaining beetroot into small cubes and set aside. In a bowl, combine the mashed potato, beetroot purée, one teaspoon of salt and a large pinch of black pepper. Beat in the egg and flour a little at a time until you have a smooth dough. It will feel a little sticky at this point. This is fine; simply dust the dough with flour until it comes away from the bowl.

3. Dust your work surface liberally with flour, tip the dough out, then divide into eight pieces and roll each piece into a long sausage shape, about 2cm (¾in) wide. Cut each roll into 2cm (¾in) pieces and coat with a little flour. Bring a large pan of salted water to the boil and add the gnocchi, in batches; boil until they float to the surface of the water. Using a slotted spoon, remove to a plate and continue with the remaining gnocchi.

4. Put the olive oil and tomatoes into a pan over a medium–high heat. Fry for 3 minutes until the tomatoes have softened and are beginning to caramelise. Add the gnocchi and the spinach and stir until the spinach wilts. Add the butter and garlic and fry for 5 minutes until aromatic. Finally, stir in the cubed beetroot and the Parmesan and heat through. Season to taste with salt and pepper. Serve immediately, with extra Parmesan on the side.

WILD MUSHROOMS WITH PARMESAN POLENTA

Polenta is dried corn that has been ground to make fine, medium or coarse cornmeal. A coarse texture works best here, producing a lovely, almost chewy texture. 'Proper' polenta takes about 50 minutes to cook, but it is far better than instant or quick-cooking varieties.

Serves 4
Prep time: 5 minutes
Cook time: 50 minutes
VEGETARIAN – see tip

300ml (½ pint) milk
700ml (1¼ pints) water
140g (5oz) medium or coarse polenta (sometimes sold as cornmeal)
4 tbsp salted butter
50g (2oz) Parmesan, grated
2 tbsp olive oil
400g (14oz) mixed wild mushrooms, thickly sliced
small handful of flat-leaf parsley, roughly chopped
sea salt and black pepper

1. Put the milk, water and cornmeal into a large high-sided pan over a high heat. Bring to the boil, whisking frequently to ensure there are no lumps. Once it has come to a rolling boil, whisk continuously for 3–5 minutes, or until the mixture has become noticeably thicker. Reduce the heat to low and simmer very gently for 45 minutes, stirring every 3–4 minutes to prevent it from catching on the bottom. If the mixture is still spitting and bubbling, the heat is too high and should be reduced even further until it is very gently simmering.

2. When the mixture is pulling away from the sides of the pan and is thick and creamy, stir in the butter and most of the Parmesan. Season to taste with three-quarters to one teaspoon of salt.

3. About 10 minutes before the polenta is done, put the olive oil into a pan over a high heat. Add the mushrooms to the pan and fry for 4–6 minutes, until golden. Stir in most of the parsley and season to taste with salt and pepper.

4. Serve the polenta with the mushrooms on top, and the remaining Parmesan and parsley scattered over.

Tips
If you really are stuck for time, mashed potato with plenty of butter and Parmesan is a quicker alternative to the polenta and does not need frequent stirring.

If you are vegetarian, look for vegetarian Italian-style hard cheese, as Parmesan is made with animal rennet.

Instead of wild mushrooms, you could use a mixture of shiitake and Portobello mushrooms.

JOLLOF RICE WITH PLANTAIN

This spicy African rice dish is a great one-pan dinner, served here with golden, slightly sweet plantain.

Best of
HOME
COOK

Serves 6–8
Prep time: 5 minutes
Cook time: 30 minutes
VEGETARIAN – see tip

400ml (14fl oz) tomato passata
3 tbsp tomato purée
2 fresh red Scotch bonnet chillies, de-seeded
2 onions, chopped
2 red peppers, de-seeded and roughly chopped
8 garlic cloves, peeled
3 tbsp fresh rosemary leaves
1 tbsp fresh thyme leaves
2 tsp ground coriander
1½ tsp sweet smoked paprika
50ml (2fl oz) olive oil
150g (5oz) cherry tomatoes, halved
800ml (28fl oz) chicken stock
2 bay leaves
500g (1lb 2oz) long grain rice, rinsed until water runs clear
2 tbsp sunflower oil
2 ripe plantains, peeled and thickly sliced
small handful of coriander leaves, roughly chopped
sea salt and black pepper
green salad, to serve

1. Put the tomato passata, tomato purée, Scotch bonnets, onions, red peppers, garlic, rosemary, thyme, ground coriander and smoked paprika into a blender or food processor and blitz until smooth.

2. Heat the olive oil in a large pan (with a lid) over a medium heat. Add the cherry tomatoes and the blitzed sauce, bring to the boil, then reduce the heat slightly and simmer for 5 minutes, stirring occasionally.

3. Add the stock, bay leaves, rice, one and a half teaspoons of salt and a large pinch of black pepper and stir to combine. Bring to the boil, then reduce the heat and simmer for 10–12 minutes, stirring frequently to prevent the rice from sticking and burning, until the rice is cooked through. Turn off the heat, cover with the lid and leave to steam for 15 minutes without removing the lid.

4. Meanwhile, heat the sunflower oil in a pan over a medium heat. Fry the plantain for a few minutes on each side until golden and soft.

5. Serve the rice with the plantain and coriander scattered over and a green salad on the side.

Tip
If you are vegetarian, replace the chicken stock with vegetable stock.

CRISPY FRIED RICE WITH PRAWNS & GREEN BEANS

This is an ideal way to use up leftover rice; alternatively, you can use the pouches of pre-cooked rice available in supermarkets. If using leftover rice, avoid using any that has already been reheated. It is a good idea to have everything ready to go before you heat up the pan.

Serves 4
Prep time: 10 minutes
Cook time: 10 minutes

4 tbsp vegetable oil
300g (10½oz) peeled raw tiger prawns
150g (5oz) green beans, trimmed
5 garlic cloves, crushed
5cm (2in) piece of fresh root ginger, peeled and finely grated
2 tbsp soy sauce
1 tbsp fish sauce, or extra soy sauce
2 limes: grated zest and 3 tbsp juice
2 fresh red chillies, halved lengthways, de-seeded and thinly sliced
800g (1¾lb) cooked and cooled jasmine rice
a handful of unsalted roasted peanuts or cashew nuts
small handful of coriander leaves
sea salt and black pepper

1. Heat the oil in a large wok or pan over a high heat. Once extremely hot, add the prawns, green beans, garlic, ginger, soy sauce, fish sauce, lime zest and juice and most of the chilli, and stir-fry for 2–3 minutes until the prawns are almost cooked. Keep everything moving all the time so as not to burn the garlic.

2. Add the rice and mix thoroughly. Spread the rice over the base of the pan and fry for 1 minute, then toss together. Repeat this process a few more times until the rice begins to crisp up. This may take a little longer with freshly cooked rice as it contains more moisture.

3. Season to taste with salt and pepper. Don't use more soy sauce as this will result in the rice being less crispy. Serve immediately, with the remaining chilli, roasted nuts and coriander scattered over.

Tip
Leftover cooked rice should be cooled and refrigerated immediately, and kept for no longer than 2 days.

CHICKEN BIRYANI

This Indian all-in-one dish is full of aromatic flavours and spices, and is delicious served with a crunchy fresh salad.

Serves 6–8
Prep time: 15 minutes
Cook time: 40 minutes

60g (2½oz) flaked almonds
4 tbsp sunflower oil
2 potatoes, about 150g (5oz) each,
    peeled and diced
1 onion, finely chopped
5 cardamom pods
2 cinnamon sticks
1 star anise
1 tbsp cumin seeds
2 bay leaves
4 boneless skinless chicken thighs,
    cut into bite-sized pieces
5 tbsp tomato purée
5 tbsp natural Greek-style yoghurt
100g (4oz) frozen peas
5 garlic cloves, crushed
1 green chilli, de-seeded, finely sliced
1 red chilli, de-seeded, finely sliced
2 tsp mild chilli powder
1 tbsp garam masala
1½ tsp ground turmeric
pinch of saffron threads (optional)
350g (12oz) basmati rice, rinsed well
1 litre (1¾ pints) chicken stock
1 tsp fine sea salt
4 eggs
2 tbsp unsalted butter
large handful of coriander leaves,
    finely chopped
1 lime, cut into wedges

1. Preheat the oven to 200°C/180°C fan/gas 6.

2. Scatter the flaked almonds on a baking sheet and roast in the oven for 3–4 minutes, until golden and aromatic

3. Heat the oil in a large pan (with a tight-fitting lid) over a medium heat. Add the potatoes, onion, cardamom, cinnamon, star anise, cumin seeds and bay leaves and sauté for 10 minutes, stirring frequently, until the onion is soft and translucent.

4. Add the chicken, tomato purée, yoghurt, peas, garlic, most of the green and red chilli, the chilli powder, garam masala, turmeric and saffron, and cook for 5 minutes until sizzling and aromatic.

5. Stir in the rice, stock and salt, bring to the boil, then reduce the heat slightly and simmer for 8–10 minutes, stirring frequently to prevent the rice from sticking and burning, until all but a few tablespoons of stock has been absorbed. Turn off the heat, cover with the lid and leave to steam for 10 minutes, without removing the lid.

6. Meanwhile, boil the eggs for 6 minutes, then transfer to a bowl of cold water and leave to cool for a few minutes before peeling. Cut in half or quarters.

7. Stir the butter and most of the coriander through the rice. Serve with the boiled eggs, roasted almonds, and the remaining coriander and chilli scattered over and with the lime wedges on the side.

Best of
HOME
COOK

RISOTTO PRIMAVERA

A risotto to celebrate the new season of spring vegetables – asparagus, broad beans and peas.

Serves 3–4
Prep time: 15 minutes
Cook time: 45 minutes
VEGETARIAN – see tip

1 tbsp olive oil
75g (3oz) unsalted butter
½ onion, very finely chopped
1 celery stick, very finely chopped
1 small carrot, very finely chopped
1 garlic clove, crushed
120g (4½oz) asparagus spears
750ml (about 1¼ pints) vegetable stock
175g (6oz) risotto rice, such as Arborio or carnaroli
50ml (2fl oz) dry white wine
100g (4oz) double-podded broad beans
75g (3oz) petits pois
40g (1½oz) Parmesan, finely grated
1 mint sprig, leaves finely chopped
1 dill sprig, finely chopped
1 parsley sprig, leaves finely chopped
sea salt and black pepper

1. Heat the olive oil and 50g (2oz) of the butter in a heavy-based pan. Add the onion, celery, carrot and garlic and cook over a low heat, stirring occasionally, for 10 minutes until soft but not coloured.

2. Meanwhile, snap the woody ends from the asparagus spears and discard, then slice each spear on the diagonal into 3–4cm (about 1½in) pieces. Pour the stock into a separate pan and bring to a simmer.

3. Add the rice to the softened vegetables and stir until coated in the butter and oil. Cook for a few minutes, then pour in the wine and keep stirring for 1–2 minutes until the liquid has evaporated.

4. Add the vegetable stock one ladleful at a time, stirring until all the liquid has been absorbed before adding more stock.

5. Towards the end of cooking (about 3–4 minutes), before you finish the stock, add the broad beans and peas to the rice and season with salt and pepper. At the same time, drop the asparagus into the remaining stock and simmer until al dente, then lift out using a slotted spoon and add to the rice.

6. Continue cooking until all the stock has been absorbed and the rice grains are al dente. Take the pan off the heat and stir in 25g (1oz) of the grated Parmesan and the remaining butter. Put the lid on the pan and leave for 5 minutes. Stir in the chopped herbs. Spoon onto serving plates and scatter over the remaining Parmesan. Serve immediately.

Tips
If you are vegetarian, look for vegetarian Italian-style hard cheese, as Parmesan is made with animal rennet.

If you are not keen on dill, replace with extra parsley.

COUSCOUS WITH COURGETTE, HALOUMI & GARLIC YOGHURT

Couscous is very quick to prepare, so it's a great grain to have on standby. Other vegetables also work well with couscous (see tip), and the garlic yoghurt brings it all together.

Serves 4
Prep time: 10 minutes
Cook time: 10–15 minutes
VEGETARIAN

320g (11oz) couscous
400ml (14fl oz) boiling water
5 tbsp extra-virgin olive oil
1 courgette, halved lengthways
    and roughly chopped
250g (9oz) haloumi cheese, cut into
    2cm (¾in) pieces
30g (1oz) fresh mint leaves,
    roughly chopped
20g (¾oz) fresh parsley leaves,
    roughly chopped
100g (4oz) cherry tomatoes, halved
1 tbsp balsamic vinegar
2 tbsp pomegranate seeds
sea salt and black pepper

For the garlic yoghurt
250g (9oz) natural yoghurt
2 garlic cloves, crushed
pinch of sea salt and black pepper

1. For the garlic yoghurt, combine all of the ingredients in a bowl and set aside.

2. Put the couscous into a large wide bowl. Stir half a teaspoon of sea salt into the boiling water and pour over the couscous. Leave to soak for 5–10 minutes, then fluff with a fork and stir in three tablespoons of the olive oil.

3. While the couscous is soaking, add another tablespoon of olive oil to a large pan and place over a high heat. Add the courgette and fry for 4–5 minutes until golden and slightly charred in places. Season with salt and pepper to taste and remove to a bowl. Add the haloumi to the pan and fry for 2–3 minutes until golden underneath, then turn and cook for a further 4–5 minutes, stirring occasionally.

4. Add most of the chopped herbs to the couscous, along with the tomatoes, courgette and haloumi, and mix. Stir in the balsamic vinegar and another tablespoon of extra-virgin olive oil. Taste and adjust the seasoning if necessary.

5. Serve on a large dish with the remaining herbs and pomegranate seeds scattered over and the garlic yoghurt dolloped on top.

Tip
Instead of the courgette, you could use a red or yellow pepper, an aubergine or Brussels sprouts.

ROASTED AUBERGINE, BULGUR, FETA & OLIVES

Bulgur wheat has a lovely nutty flavour and chewy consistency and is quick and easy to cook.

Serves 4
Prep time: 10 minutes
Cook time: 25–30 minutes
VEGETARIAN
VEGAN – see tip

2 aubergines, cut into
    bite-sized pieces
4 tbsp olive oil
5 tbsp balsamic vinegar
160g (5½oz) bulgur wheat
2 tbsp extra-virgin olive oil
50g (2oz) pine nuts
150g (5oz) cherry tomatoes, halved
75g (3oz) feta, crumbled
60g (2½oz) pitted mixed olives,
    roughly chopped
large handful of flat-leaf parsley
    leaves, chopped
sea salt and black pepper

1. Preheat the oven to 200°C/180°C fan/gas 6.

2. Put the aubergines into a roasting tin, toss with the olive oil and three tablespoons of the balsamic vinegar, season well with salt and pepper and roast for 25–30 minutes, until the aubergines are deep golden and tender.

3. Meanwhile, bring a pan of salted water to the boil, add the bulgur wheat and simmer for 10–15 minutes until tender. Drain and, while still hot, stir in the remaining two tablespoons of balsamic vinegar and the extra-virgin olive oil. Season to taste with salt and pepper.

4. Shortly before the aubergines have finished cooking, scatter the pine nuts on a baking sheet and roast in the oven for 3–4 minutes, until golden and aromatic.

5. Combine the bulgur with the roasted aubergine, the tomatoes, feta, olives and parsley. Taste and adjust the seasoning if necessary. Serve on a large platter and scatter over the roasted pine nuts.

Tip
If you are avoiding dairy, you can omit the feta and add a few more olives.

PEARL BARLEY, PEACH, BROCCOLI & CRISPY BREAD

The subtle sweetness of peaches goes really well with the spicy harissa and earthy barley.

Serves 4
Prep time: 5 minutes
Cook time: 25–30 minutes
VEGETARIAN

200g (7oz) raw pearl barley,
    or 400g (14oz) cooked pearl
    barley (available in packs in
    supermarkets)
2 tbsp harissa paste
1 lemon: grated zest and 1 tbsp juice
300g (10½oz) broccoli florets or
    tenderstem broccoli
5 tbsp extra-virgin olive oil
3 thick slices of sourdough
    or rustic bread, cut into
    bite-sized pieces
3 peaches or nectarines, stoned
    and cut into wedges
large handful of flat-leaf parsley,
    roughly chopped
sea salt and black pepper

1. Preheat the oven to 220°c/200°c fan/gas 7.

2. If using raw pearl barley, bring a pan of salted water to the boil, add the barley and simmer briskly for 25–30 minutes until the barley is cooked through but still al dente. Drain and, while still hot, stir in the harissa, lemon zest and juice. Season to taste with salt and pepper. If using cooked pearl barley, heat it gently in a pan with a tablespoon or two of water. Once warm, stir in the harissa and lemon zest and juice and season to taste.

3. Meanwhile, toss the broccoli with one tablespoon of the olive oil and season well with salt and pepper. Roast for 10–15 minutes until slightly charred and cooked through.

4. Heat two tablespoons of the oil in a pan over a medium heat. Add the bread and fry for 5–7 minutes until golden and crisp. Remove from the heat and season with salt and pepper.

5. Combine the barley with the broccoli, bread, peaches or nectarines, parsley and two tablespoons of oil. Taste and adjust the seasoning if necessary. Serve on a large platter.

POULTRY & GAME

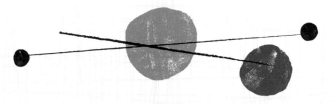

CHICKEN, CHORIZO & SWEET POTATO BAKE

Pan-frying the chicken for a few minutes before roasting gives the skin a lovely crispiness and golden colour, but if you are stuck for time you can skip this step.

Serves 4
Prep time: 10 minutes
Cook time: 50 minutes

2 tbsp olive oil
8 chicken thighs, skin on
150g (5oz) chorizo,
    chopped into chunks
1 red onion, thinly sliced
2 sweet potatoes, cut into wedges
    (no need to peel)
1 orange
a handful of rosemary leaves
1 tsp dried chilli flakes
sea salt and black pepper

1. Preheat the oven to 200°C/180°C fan/gas 6.

2. Heat one tablespoon of the olive oil in a large pan over a medium–high heat. Season the chicken thighs with salt and pepper, then place them into the hot pan, skin side down. Fry for 5–6 minutes, or until golden and crisp, then turn and fry on the other side for another 3–4 minutes.

3. Transfer to a roasting tin, skin side up, with the chorizo, red onion and sweet potato. Using a vegetable peeler, peel strips of zest off the orange and add them to the tin, together with the rosemary, chilli flakes and remaining tablespoon of oil. Season with salt and pepper and gently combine everything together. Bake for 35–40 minutes, or until the chicken and sweet potato are cooked through. Serve immediately.

CHICKEN KIEV

The classic combination of parsley, garlic and butter really makes this dish, but you could use basil instead, and if you like spice, some dried chilli flakes give a delicious kick.

Serves 4
Prep time: 30 minutes, plus chilling
Cook time: 18 minutes

75g (3oz) unsalted butter, at room temperature
3 garlic cloves, crushed
4 tbsp finely chopped flat-leaf parsley leaves
4 boneless skinless chicken breasts (not previously frozen)
75g (3oz) plain flour, plus extra for mixing if needed
2 eggs, beaten
150g (5oz) fresh breadcrumbs
sunflower oil, for frying
sea salt and black pepper
mashed potatoes and green vegetables, such as broccoli, to serve

1. In a bowl, beat the butter, garlic and parsley together until evenly combined. Season with a good pinch of salt and pepper. Transfer to a sheet of clingfilm and roll into a sausage shape, then place in the freezer for 15 minutes.

2. Meanwhile, butterfly each chicken breast: place on a chopping board and use a sharp knife to slice into the thicker side; holding the knife parallel to the board, slice across the breast horizontally, taking care not to cut all the way through, until you can open it out like a book. Then place each chicken breast between two sheets of clingfilm and bash with a rolling pin until completely flattened, taking care not to tear the chicken or create any holes.

3. Unwrap and divide the frozen butter into four pieces. Place one on each chicken breast, then wrap the flesh around the butter to fully enclose it. If you like, mix a little flour with water to create a paste to help stick the chicken in place. Place the chicken in the freezer for 15 minutes to firm up.

4. Preheat the oven to 200°C/180°C fan/gas 6.

5. Put the flour, beaten egg and breadcrumbs in separate bowls. Carefully coat the chicken breasts first in the flour, then in the beaten egg and finally in the breadcrumbs.

6. Fill a large deep pan with oil to a depth of 2cm (¾in) and place over a medium–high heat. Test the oil is hot enough by dropping in a small piece of bread: it should brown in 50 seconds. Place the chicken into the pan, seam side down, and fry for 6 minutes, turning now and again, until it is golden and crisp all over.

7. Put the chicken into a roasting in. Bake for 12 minutes or until cooked through. Serve immediately, with mash and green veg.

SPICED ROAST CHICKEN

This punchy marinade is sure to liven up your roast chicken and, with its coconut milk base, creates a lovely spicy citrus gravy.

Best of **HOME COOK**

Serves 4
Prep time: 15 minutes
Cook time: 1¾ hours, plus resting

1½ lemons
2 onions, peeled and cut into wedges
1 orange, cut into wedges (unpeeled)
400ml (14fl oz) coconut milk
500ml (17fl oz) chicken stock
2 bay leaves
1 small chicken, about 1.2kg (2½lb)
1 clementine
a handful of coriander leaves
2 tbsp unsalted butter
1 tsp cornflour
sea salt and black pepper

For the marinade
2½ tsp mild (Kashmiri) chilli powder
1 tbsp ground cumin
1 tbsp ground coriander
1 tbsp ground turmeric
1 tsp garam masala
1 tsp fresh thyme leaves
2 tbsp runny honey
1 tsp sea salt
1 tbsp Worcestershire sauce
5 tbsp natural yoghurt
1 tsp white wine vinegar
2 garlic cloves, crushed
50g (2oz) piece of fresh root ginger,
    peeled and finely grated
1 tbsp tomato purée
100g (4oz) unsalted butter, melted
2 tbsp olive oil

1. Preheat the oven to 200°C/180°C fan/gas 6. You will need a large roasting tin and a wire rack that will fit inside, for the chicken to sit on.

2. Boil one lemon in water for 20 minutes until soft and set aside.

3. Combine all the marinade ingredients in a bowl and set aside.

4. Put the onion and orange wedges, coconut milk, stock and bay leaves into the roasting tin. Cut up the remaining half lemon into chunks and add. Put the rack inside the roasting tin and place the chicken on top.

5. Using a sharp knife, score the legs and breast of the chicken. Massage the marinade into the chicken and inside the cavity (plastic gloves are useful for this). Stab the boiled lemon a few times and place in the cavity, together with the clementine and the fresh coriander.

6. Roast the chicken for 1 hour 15–25 minutes, basting every 30 minutes or so, until dark golden and cooked through: the juices should run clear when the thickest part of the thigh is pierced with a skewer. The spice marinade can darken considerably, so if the chicken is browning too quickly for your liking, cover with foil. Remove from the oven, cover and leave to rest for 20–30 minutes.

7. To make the gravy, pour the entire contents of the roasting tin into a blender or food processor and blitz until almost smooth. Pass the mixture though a fine sieve into a jug. Melt the butter in a pan over a medium heat, whisk in the cornflour, then immediately pour in the blended mixture a little at a time, whisking constantly. Season to taste with salt and pepper.

8. Serve the gravy alongside the chicken. Golden Bombay Potatoes (page 71) and Cumin and Clementine Spiced Carrots (page 70) are ideal side dishes here.

MUSTARD CHICKEN & FENNEL CASSEROLE

Full of Mediterranean flavours, warm and comforting, this recipe consists of mostly hands-off cooking time, so you can be getting on with something else while it simmers its way to perfection.

Serves 4–6
Prep time: 10 minutes
Cook time: 1 hour 20 minutes

8 chicken thighs, skin on
2 tbsp olive oil
2 red onions, thinly sliced
1 tsp ground cumin
1 tsp ground coriander
1 tsp dried chilli flakes
5 garlic cloves, crushed
2 fennel bulbs, tough outer leaves removed, cut into wedges
2 tbsp wholegrain mustard
500ml (17fl oz) chicken or vegetable stock
1 × 400g tin peeled plum tomatoes
2 bay leaves
2 sprigs of rosemary, leaves removed
small handful of flat-leaf parsley leaves, roughly chopped
extra-virgin olive oil, to drizzle
sea salt and black pepper
crusty bread or cooked rice, to serve

1. Season the chicken with salt and pepper. Heat the olive oil in a large deep pan (with a lid) over a medium–high heat. In batches, add the chicken, skin side down, and fry for 3–4 minutes until deep golden brown, then turn and fry on the other side for another 3–4 minutes; remove and set aside while you cook the remaining chicken. Discard most of the residual oil, leaving about one tablespoon.

2. Add the onions, cumin, coriander and chilli flakes and sauté over a medium heat for about 8 minutes until the onions are soft. Add the garlic and fry for another 2 minutes until aromatic.

3. Put the chicken back into the pan, together with the fennel, mustard, stock, tomatoes, bay leaves, rosemary leaves, half a teaspoon of salt and a grinding of black pepper. Bear in mind that you may need less salt if your stock was already salted.

4. Bring to the boil, then reduce the heat to low, cover with the lid and simmer gently for 1 hour until the fennel and chicken are meltingly tender.

5. Taste and adjust the seasoning if necessary. Stir through the parsley, drizzle over a little extra-virgin olive oil and serve with some crusty bread or cooked rice to mop up all of the delicious juices.

CHICKEN, MUSHROOM & COCKLE PIE

The cockles add a lovely taste of the sea to this pie, and they are quite easy to find in good supermarkets. However, this works just as well without the cockles, if you prefer.

Serves 4
Prep time: 15 minutes
Cook time: 55 minutes

25g (1oz) unsalted butter
1 shallot, finely sliced
150g (5oz) smoked streaky bacon, diced
2 garlic cloves, crushed
75–90g (about 3–3½oz) mixed dried mushrooms, soaked in boiling water for 20 minutes
200g (7oz) mixed fresh mushrooms, thinly sliced
300g (10½oz) boneless skinless chicken thighs, cut into bite-sized pieces
40g (1½oz) plain flour
300ml (½ pint) chicken stock
150ml (¼ pint) single cream
100g (4oz) Wensleydale cheese, grated
100g (4oz) fresh shelled cockles
a handful of parsley, roughly chopped
375g (13oz) ready-rolled puff pastry
1 egg, beaten
sea salt and black pepper

1. Preheat the oven to 200°c/180°c fan/gas 6.

2. Melt the butter in a large deep pan over a medium heat. Add the shallot and bacon and fry for 8 minutes until the shallot has softened and the bacon is crisp. Add the garlic and fry for another 1–2 minutes until aromatic.

3. Drain the soaked mushrooms and add them to the pan, together with the fresh mushrooms and chicken, then fry for 10 minutes until browned all over.

4. Stir in the flour until combined, then increase the heat to high and add the stock, cream, cheese, cockles and parsley and stir to combine. Season to taste with a little salt and pepper, bearing in mind the bacon will have provided some salt. Remove from the heat and leave to cool a little.

5. Transfer the mixture to a large pie dish. Place the puff pastry on top and press it onto the rim of the dish, then trim the edge using a sharp knife. If you wish, decorate the top with pastry trimmings and crimp the edges with a fork. Brush the pastry with beaten egg and season with a little salt and pepper.

6. Bake for 30–35 minutes until the pastry is risen, crisp and golden. Serve immediately.

CHICKEN TIKKA MASALA

This is one of those dishes that tastes even better the day after it was made, and it also freezes well, so if you wish you can double the recipe and freeze half.

Serves 4
Prep time: 10 minutes
Cook time: 30 minutes

4 tbsp ghee or sunflower oil
800g (1¾lb) boneless skinless chicken breasts and thighs, cut into bite-sized pieces
3 tsp garam masala
1 tsp ground turmeric
2 onions, finely chopped
2 tsp finely grated fresh root ginger
6 garlic cloves, crushed
1 tsp ground cumin
1 tsp sweet smoked paprika
2 tbsp tomato purée
1 × 400g tin chopped tomatoes
200g (7oz) natural yoghurt
100ml (3½fl oz) double cream
1 tbsp fresh lemon juice
small handful of coriander leaves
sea salt and black pepper
cooked rice and/or naan bread, to serve

1. Heat half the ghee or oil in a large pan over a medium–high heat. Add the chicken, half the garam masala and turmeric, one teaspoon of salt and half a teaspoon of pepper. Toss everything together and fry for 6–8 minutes until golden and cooked through. Remove to a bowl and set aside; return the pan to the heat.

2. Add the remaining ghee or oil and the onions to the pan and fry for 6–8 minutes until translucent. Add the ginger and garlic, reduce the heat to medium and fry for a further 5 minutes until aromatic. Add the remaining garam masala and turmeric, together with the cumin, smoked paprika, tomato purée and chopped tomatoes, bring to the boil, then reduce the heat and simmer for 5 minutes.

3. Stir in the yoghurt, cream and lemon juice. Taste and adjust the seasoning with more salt and pepper. At this point you can purée the sauce in a blender or food processor, or simply leave it as it is. Stir the cooked chicken back into the sauce and warm through.

4. Serve immediately with the coriander scattered over and the rice and/or naan bread on the side.

ROAST PHEASANT, BROCCOLI & NEW POTATOES

If you are keen to try cooking game birds at home, pheasant is a good place to start: it's inexpensive to buy and widely available, and not overly gamey in flavour. Here, everything is cooked in one roasting tin, making it easily achievable.

Serves 4
Prep time: 10 minutes
Cook time: 55 minutes,
    plus resting

4 tbsp olive oil
2 pheasants, roughly 800g (1¾lb)
    each, preferably hen pheasants
800g (1¾lb) new potatoes, halved
    (no need to peel)
4 rosemary sprigs, leaves removed
500g (1lb 2oz) broccoli florets or
    tenderstem broccoli
sea salt and black pepper
green salad, to serve (optional)

1. Preheat the oven to 190°C/170°C fan/gas 5.

2. Pour two tablespoons of the olive oil into a large pan and place over a medium heat. Season the pheasants all over with salt and pepper, then add them to the pan and fry until golden brown on all sides; this will take about 10 minutes, and a pair of tongs is useful for turning the birds.

3. Put the potatoes into a large roasting tin, toss with the remaining two tablespoons of oil and the rosemary leaves, and season well with salt and pepper. Add the pheasants, breast side up, and roast for 30 minutes.

4. Add the broccoli, toss with the potatoes and season with salt and pepper. Turn the pheasants so they are breast side down. Roast for a further 15 minutes until the potatoes, broccoli and pheasants are cooked through. Remove from the oven, cover with foil and leave to rest for 15 minutes.

5. Turn the birds breast side up and place the entire roasting tin on the table, ready to carve, or plate up individually. A green salad would be a nice accompaniment here.

CHICKEN BALLOTINE

This is a classic dish of chicken thighs stuffed with a chicken and mushroom mousse, which are poached and then pan-fried. It is lovely served with some simple greens fried in butter.

Best of
HOME
COOK

Serves 4
Prep time: 20 minutes
Cook time: 35 minutes, plus resting

3 tbsp olive oil
1 small onion, very finely chopped
100g (4oz) fresh shiitake mushrooms, finely chopped
130g (4½oz) boneless skinless chicken breast
1 tbsp fresh thyme leaves
90ml (3fl oz) double cream
4 boneless skinless chicken thighs
1 tbsp snipped fresh chives (optional)
sea salt and black pepper
pan-fried greens, to serve

1. Heat two tablespoons of the oil in a frying pan over a medium heat. Add the onion and mushrooms and sauté for 8–10 minutes until softened.

2. Put the chicken breast, thyme and the onion and mushroom mixture into a food processor and blitz until finely ground. With the machine running, pour in the cream until you have a mousse. Season with half a teaspoon of salt and a grinding of pepper.

3. Place the chicken thighs between two sheets of clingfilm and flatten with a rolling pin. Season the thighs with a pinch of salt and pepper. Divide the mousse between the four chicken thighs, then roll up the thigh meat, encasing the mousse. Tightly wrap each roll in clingfilm, twisting the ends of the clingfilm to keep everything in place.

4. Bring a pan of water to a gentle simmer. Add the clingfilm-wrapped chicken and poach gently for 20 minutes, ensuring the water does not come to the boil, otherwise the chicken will be tough.

5. Remove from the pan and leave to rest for 5 minutes, then remove the clingfilm. Put the remaining tablespoon of olive oil into a pan and place over a medium–high heat. Add the chicken rolls and fry for 5 minutes, turning now and again, until golden brown all over.

6. Cut the ballotines into thick slices and serve with the chives scattered over (if wished) and some pan-fried greens on the side.

SEARED DUCK WITH CHICKPEAS, COURGETTE & ROCKET

This is a great dish to make for a dinner party (see tip), as you can cook the duck breasts shortly before your guests arrive, leaving them to rest while you prepare the chickpeas and courgette. You can save the rendered duck fat for cooking roast potatoes.

Serves 2
Prep time: 10 minutes
Cook time: 30 minutes, plus resting

2 duck breasts, skin on
2 tbsp olive oil
1 × 400g tin chickpeas, drained and rinsed
1 courgette, halved lengthways and thickly sliced
2 garlic cloves, crushed
100g (4oz) rocket
extra-virgin olive oil, to drizzle
sea salt and black pepper

1. Preheat the oven to 200°c/180°c fan/gas 6.

2. Score the skin of the duck breasts about eight times with a sharp knife, ensuring you do not cut deeply into the flesh. Pat dry with kitchen paper and season with salt and pepper. Place the duck breasts, skin side down, on a dry ovenproof frying pan over a medium heat. Fry for 6–8 minutes, keeping the breasts skin side down. Pour the fat out of the pan as it renders, keeping the pan as dry as possible.

3. Once the skin is golden brown and the majority of the fat has rendered, turn the duck breasts skin side up and transfer the pan to the oven; cook for 10–12 minutes, depending on how pink you like your duck. Once cooked, remove from the oven, cover with foil and leave to rest for 20 minutes.

4. Meanwhile, heat the olive oil in a pan over a medium–high heat. Add the chickpeas and courgette and fry for 6–8 minutes until golden and the chickpeas are slightly crisp. Add the garlic and fry for another 2 minutes until aromatic. Remove from the heat and season well with salt and pepper.

5. When the duck breasts have rested, slice them thickly at an angle. Combine the chickpeas and courgette with the rocket and divide between two plates. Top with the sliced duck and drizzle over a little extra-virgin olive oil. Serve immediately.

Tip
To make this dish for six people, simply scale up, using 6 duck breasts, 4–6 tablespoons of olive oil, 3 tins of chickpeas, 3 courgettes, 5–6 garlic cloves and 300g (10½oz) rocket.

CHICKEN WITH CREAMY MUSHROOM SAUCE

This mushroom sauce is rich, with a real depth of flavour that is delicious with the chicken and broccoli. You can make it a day in advance and reheat when ready to serve the chicken.

Best of
HOME
COOK

Serves 4

Prep time: 10 minutes

Cook time: 45 minutes

2 tbsp unsalted butter

3 tbsp olive oil

350g (12oz) chestnut mushrooms, thinly sliced

1 onion, finely chopped

2 garlic cloves, crushed

1 tbsp fresh thyme leaves

1 tsp ground coriander

1 tsp ground cumin

100ml (3½fl oz) dry white wine

300ml (½ pint) chicken stock

150ml (¼ pint) double cream

100g (4oz) crème fraîche

1 tbsp Dijon mustard

small handful of flat-leaf parsley leaves, finely chopped

small handful of tarragon leaves, finely chopped

4 chicken breasts, skin on

sea salt and black pepper

tenderstem broccoli and cooked rice, to serve

1. Heat the butter and two tablespoons of the olive oil in a pan over a medium heat. Add the mushrooms and onion and sauté for 10–12 minutes, stirring frequently, until the mushrooms are golden and the onions are softened. Add the garlic, thyme, ground coriander and cumin and fry for another 2 minutes until aromatic.

2. Turn up the heat, pour in the wine and boil for 1 minute. Add the chicken stock, double cream, crème fraîche and mustard and bring to the boil. Reduce the heat and simmer for 5 minutes to thicken. Stir through most of the parsley and tarragon and season to taste with salt and pepper. Set aside.

3. For the chicken, preheat the oven to 180°C/160°C fan/gas 4. Place a heavy ovenproof frying pan over a high heat and add the remaining one tablespoon of oil. Season the chicken breasts and fry, skin-side down, for 5 minutes until golden brown. Put the pan into the oven for 10–15 minutes until the chicken is cooked through. Remove from the oven, cover with baking parchment and leave to rest for 6–7 minutes.

4. To serve, gently reheat the sauce if necessary and then divide the sauce between four wide shallow bowls. Slice the chicken thickly at an angle and place on top of the sauce. Scatter over the remaining herbs. Serve immediately, with rice and broccoli on the side.

PORK, LAMB & BEEF

SAUSAGE, FENNEL & TOMATO BAKE

This simple one-pan dinner is a great way to use up stale bread, although fresh crusty bread can also be used. The bread becomes crispy on the outside and chewy in the middle, having soaked up all the wonderful cooking juices.

Serves 4
Prep time: 10 minutes
Cook time: 1 hour

2 fennel bulbs, tough outer
    leaves removed
6 tbsp olive oil
300g (10½oz) cherry tomatoes
2 red onions, cut into thin wedges
2 thick slices of bread, cut into
    bite-sized pieces
8 pork sausages
1 tsp cumin seeds
1 tbsp fresh thyme leaves
3 tbsp water
sea salt and black pepper

1. Preheat the oven to 190°C/170°C fan/gas 5.

2. Cut the fennel bulbs in half and then into 2cm (¾in) wedges. Put them into a large roasting tin and toss with two tablespoons of the olive oil. Season well with salt and pepper and roast for 20 minutes.

3. Add the tomatoes, onions, bread, sausages, cumin, thyme, water and the remaining four tablespoons of olive oil. Season with salt and pepper, mix everything together and return to the oven to roast for 20 minutes.

4. Remove from the oven, stir well, turn the sausages over and roast for a final 20 minutes until the fennel and onions are tender – a small sharp knife should glide easily into them – and the sausages are golden and cooked through. Serve immediately.

SAUSAGES & HORSERADISH MASH WITH RED ONION GRAVY

Horseradish adds a lovely mustardy kick to mashed potato, but you can leave it out if you prefer plain mash. The red onion gravy is rich, delicious and well worth the effort.

Serves 4
Prep time: 10 minutes
Cook time: 30 minutes

1kg (2lb 3oz) floury potatoes
    (such as Maris Piper),
    peeled and quartered
4 tbsp salted butter
6 tbsp milk or cream
2 tbsp creamed horseradish
    (from a jar), or more to taste
3 tbsp olive oil
3 red onions, thinly sliced
3 rosemary sprigs, leaves
    removed and chopped
4 garlic cloves, crushed
4 tbsp balsamic vinegar
1 tsp runny honey
400ml (14fl oz) chicken or
    vegetable stock
1 tbsp cornflour
8 pork sausages
sea salt and black pepper

1. Cook the potatoes in boiling salted water for 15–20 minutes until tender. Drain and return to the pan to steam dry for a few minutes. Mash until smooth with the butter, milk or cream and the horseradish. Season to taste with plenty of salt and pepper.

2. While the potatoes are cooking, put the olive oil into a large pan and place over a medium–low heat. Add the onions, rosemary and garlic and gently fry for 10 minutes until the onions are soft and translucent. Add the balsamic vinegar and honey and cook for another 5 minutes until slightly caramelised.

3. Stir a few tablespoons of the stock with the cornflour to form a smooth paste. Pour this and the remaining stock into the pan and stir well. Bring to the boil, then reduce the heat and simmer for 5–10 minutes until thickened. Taste and adjust the seasoning.

4. Fry or grill the sausages until golden and cooked through. Dollop some mash onto each plate, nestle the sausages into it and pour over as much of the onion gravy as you like.

SWEET & SOUR PORK WITH EGG-FRIED RICE

Best of
HOME
COOK

Making your own Chinese takeaway favourite is surprisingly easy. To make this even speedier, you can use a pouch of pre-cooked rice, available from supermarkets.

Serves 4
Prep time: 15 minutes
Cook time: 30 minutes

2 tbsp soy sauce
1 tbsp sake or dry sherry
2½ tbsp cornflour
500g (1lb 2oz) pork fillet, cut into
    2cm (¾in) cubes
2 tbsp groundnut oil
3 garlic cloves, crushed
1 onion, finely sliced
1 green pepper, de-seeded and
    finely sliced
1 carrot, finely sliced
4cm (1½in) piece of fresh root ginger,
    peeled and cut into matchsticks
3 tbsp soft brown sugar
6 tbsp rice vinegar or
    white wine vinegar
170ml (6fl oz) water
2 spring onions, finely sliced
½ fresh red chilli, de-seeded and
    finely sliced
sea salt and black pepper

For the egg-fried rice
225g (8oz) jasmine rice
2 tbsp groundnut oil
2 eggs, beaten with ½ tsp sea salt

1. In a large bowl, combine the soy sauce, sake and one tablespoon of the cornflour. Add the pork and stir to coat. Leave to stand for 10 minutes.

2. For the egg-fried rice, cook the rice according to the packet instructions. Drain, then spread out on a plate to cool.

3. Heat one tablespoon of the oil in a pan over a medium–high heat, add the pork and stir-fry for 5–7 minutes until golden brown. Remove the pork from the pan and set aside.

4. Return the pan to the heat and add another tablespoon of oil. Add the garlic, onion, green pepper, carrot and ginger and stir-fry over a medium–high heat for 2 minutes.

5. Meanwhile, in a bowl, whisk together the sugar, vinegar, water, the remaining cornflour and a pinch of salt. Add to the pan and bring to the boil, then reduce the heat slightly and simmer, stirring frequently, for 5 minutes until thickened. Remove from the heat and stir in the cooked pork. Season to taste with salt and pepper and set aside.

6. For the rice, heat the oil in a wok or large non-stick pan over a high heat. Add the cooled rice and beaten eggs and stir-fry for 4–6 minutes until some of the rice begins to colour and the egg is cooked.

7. Spoon the rice onto a serving plate and top with the pork and vegetables. Garnish with the sliced spring onions and red chilli.

BAKED HAM WITH A MAPLE & MUSTARD GLAZE

Baked ham is a classic centrepiece for any festive table. The key to a great-looking ham with a rich glaze is to leave as much of the fat intact as possible when removing the skin. The cooked ham will keep well in the fridge, ready to be sliced for a sandwich or whatever you fancy.

Serves 10–12
Prep time: 30 minutes, plus cooling
Cook time: 3 hours

4.5–5kg (10–11lb) whole leg of
    gammon, bone in
3 bay leaves
1 tsp whole black peppercorns
a handful of cloves
grated zest and juice of 1 orange
120ml (4½fl oz) maple syrup
50g (2oz) soft light brown sugar
1 tbsp wholegrain mustard
2 tsp Dijon mustard
½ tsp ground allspice
½ tsp ground cinnamon

1. Put the gammon into a very large pan with a lid, deep enough to submerge the meat in water. Add the bay leaves and peppercorns and cover with cold water. Bring to the boil, then reduce the heat, cover with a lid (leaving a small gap for the steam to escape) and simmer gently for 2 hours, topping up the water at regular intervals to ensure the meat stays submerged and removing any scum that rises to the surface.

2. After 2 hours, carefully remove the ham from the water and set aside to drain and cool for 20 minutes. Discard the cooking water or keep as a stock for soup.

3. Preheat the oven to 190°C/170°C fan/gas 5.

4. Using a small sharp knife, carefully remove the skin from the ham, leaving as much fat as possible and peeling the skin back as you go. Discard the skin. Score the fat, making a criss-cross pattern with the knife, then stud the centre of each cross with a clove. Transfer the ham into a large roasting tin lined with baking parchment.

5. In a bowl, combine the orange zest and juice, maple syrup, sugar, both mustards, allspice and cinnamon. Brush half the mixture all over the ham and roast for 30 minutes.

6. Remove from the oven and pour over the remaining mixture. Return to the oven and roast for another 25–30 minutes, generously basting the ham with the pan juices every 10 minutes, until the glaze is rich and sticky.

7. Remove from the oven and leave to cool for half an hour before slicing. Alternatively, bake the ham in advance, leave to cool completely, and serve cold.

ROAST LEG OF LAMB WITH MADEIRA GRAVY

Best of
HOME
COOK

Infused with garlic, rosemary and lemon, this roast lamb is sublime with the rich and indulgent gravy.

Serves 6–8
Prep time: 15 minutes
Cook time: 1¾ hours, plus resting

2kg (4¾lb) leg of lamb, bone in
8 garlic cloves, thickly sliced
2 rosemary sprigs, leaves removed
grated zest of 1 lemon
2 tbsp olive oil
1 onion, peeled and cut into wedges
350ml (12fl oz) Madeira
600ml (1 pint) water
40g (1½oz) unsalted butter
2 tsp cornflour
sea salt and black pepper

1. Preheat the oven to 200°C/180°C fan/gas 6.

2. Make deep incisions all over the lamb and stuff with the garlic slices and half the rosemary leaves. Rub the lemon zest and olive oil all over the surface of the lamb. Season with salt and pepper.

3. Put the onion wedges into a roasting tin, sit the lamb on top and roast for 1 hour. Pour 200ml (7fl oz) of the Madeira and half of the water into the tin and return to the oven for 30 minutes.

4. Remove from the oven, transfer the lamb to a warmed serving dish, cover with foil and leave to rest for at least 30 minutes.

5. Tip the contents of the roasting tin into a pan, together with the remaining rosemary, Madeira and water. Bring to the boil, then reduce the heat and simmer for 10 minutes until slightly reduced. Strain everything through a sieve into a jug, pressing through as much liquid as possible.

6. Melt the butter in a frying pan over a low heat. Stir in the cornflour until you have a smooth paste and cook, stirring all the time, for 1 minute. Slowly whisk in the strained liquid, a little at a time, until smooth. Simmer for 10 minutes over a low heat, stirring frequently, until thickened. Add any juices that have come out of the lamb while resting and stir well. Carve the lamb and serve with the gravy.

LANCASHIRE HOTPOT

This simple stew of lamb and onion topped with sliced potatoes would traditionally have been made with mutton, but lamb is more commonly used these days. If you want to use mutton, increase the cooking time by 30 minutes before removing the lid.

Serves 4
Prep time: 20 minutes
Cook time: 2¼ hours

800g (1¾lb) lamb neck fillet,
   cut into bite-sized pieces
2 tbsp plain flour
2 thyme sprigs
1 rosemary sprig
1 bay leaf
2 onions, roughly chopped
450ml (¾ pint) lamb or chicken stock
800g (1¾lb) floury potatoes
   (such as King Edward), peeled
2 tbsp unsalted butter, melted
sea salt and black pepper

1. Preheat the oven to 190°c/170°c fan/gas 5.

2. Put the lamb into a large casserole dish with a tight-fitting lid. Add the flour, one teaspoon of salt and half a teaspoon of freshly ground black pepper. Toss everything together until the lamb is evenly coated.

3. Add the thyme and rosemary sprigs, bay leaf and onions. Gently combine, then pour in the stock.

4. Cut the potatoes into slices 5mm (¼in) thick and arrange in an overlapping, fan-like layer on top of the meat mixture. Brush the melted butter over the potatoes, then season with salt and pepper. Cover with the lid and bake for 1¾ hours. Remove the lid and cook for a further 30 minutes, or until the potatoes are crisp and golden. Serve immediately.

SPICED LAMB SHANKS

Best of
HOME
COOK

While it does take a few hours to cook lamb shanks, the majority of this time is hands off, and you are rewarded with the most succulent and tender meat, ready to fall off the bone. These are best served with simple mashed potatoes to mix with the delicious cooking sauce.

Serves 4
Prep time: 15 minutes
Cook time: 3¼ hours

olive oil, for frying
4 lamb shanks
3 onions, finely chopped
6 garlic cloves, crushed
1 tsp mild (Kashmiri) chilli powder
1 tsp ground cumin
1 tsp ground coriander
2 rosemary sprigs, leaves removed
    and finely chopped
1 tbsp soft brown sugar
2 tbsp plain flour
2 tbsp tomato purée
1 × 400g tin chopped tomatoes
400ml (14fl oz) red wine
1 litre (1¾ pints) beef stock
small handful of flat-leaf parsley
    leaves, roughly chopped
sea salt and black pepper
mashed potato, to serve

1. Preheat the oven to 160°C/140°C fan/gas 3.

2. Heat two tablespoons of oil in a large heavy-based ovenproof pan (with a tight-fitting lid) over a medium heat. Brown the lamb shanks in batches, using more oil if needed, until browned all over. This will take 10–15 minutes. Remove to a plate.

3. Add another two tablespoons of oil and the onions to the pan and sauté over a medium heat for 8–10 minutes until soft and translucent. Add the garlic, chilli powder, cumin, coriander, rosemary, one teaspoon of salt and a good grinding of black pepper and stir-fry for 4 minutes until aromatic.

4. Stir in the sugar and flour, followed by the tomato purée, chopped tomatoes, wine and stock. Return the lamb shanks to the pan and bring the liquid to the boil, then cover with the lid and place in the oven. Cook for 2½ hours, turning the shanks now and then if not fully submerged in the liquid, until meltingly tender.

5. Carefully remove the lamb shanks to a warmed plate and cover with foil. Put the pan back over a high heat and simmer for 15 minutes, until the sauce is slightly reduced and thickened. Taste and adjust the seasoning if necessary. Stir through most of the parsley.

6. Ladle the sauce into bowls (any left over can be kept and served as gravy or sauce for another meal) and sit the lamb shanks on top. Scatter over the remaining parsley and serve with mashed potato.

MOUSSAKA

A classic moussaka, given a twist with mushrooms for added flavour, mildly spiced lamb and a creamy buffalo mozzarella topping.

Serves 4–6
Prep time: 15 minutes
Cook time: 1 hour 10 minutes

1 large aubergine,
    sliced thinly lengthways
olive oil, for frying
1 onion, thinly sliced
200g (7oz) mixed fresh mushrooms,
    roughly chopped
4 garlic cloves, crushed
500g (1lb 2oz) minced lamb
200g (7oz) cherry tomatoes, halved
1 × 400g tin chopped tomatoes
2 tbsp soy sauce
¼ tsp ground allspice
½ tsp ground cinnamon
sea salt and black pepper

For the topping
50g (2oz) unsalted butter
50g (2oz) plain flour
400ml (14fl oz) whole milk
50g (2oz) Parmesan, grated
1 egg, beaten
1 ball of buffalo mozzarella, sliced

1. Brush the aubergine with olive oil and fry (in batches if necessary) over a medium heat for 5 minutes on each side, until golden and slightly softened. Season with salt and pepper and set aside.

2. Meanwhile, put two tablespoons of olive oil into a large pan, add the onion and mushrooms and sauté for 10 minutes over a medium–high heat until the onion is softened and translucent. Add the garlic and cook for another 2 minutes until aromatic. Add the minced lamb, fresh and tinned tomatoes, soy sauce, allspice and cinnamon. Bring to the boil, then reduce the heat and simmer for 12 minutes until thickened and the mince is cooked through. Taste and adjust the seasoning if necessary.

3. Preheat the oven to 200°C/180°C fan/gas 6.

4. For the white sauce for the topping, melt the butter in a pan over a medium heat. Reduce the heat and stir in the flour until you have a smooth paste. Cook for 2 minutes, stirring constantly. Slowly stir in the milk, a little at a time, to make a smooth sauce. Simmer for 5 minutes until thickened, then reduce the heat, add most of the Parmesan and the egg and immediately whisk everything together, to prevent the egg from scrambling, until completely smooth. Continue stirring for 2 minutes, then remove from the heat and season to taste with salt and pepper.

5. Put the mince mixture into a large baking dish. Lay the aubergine slices on top. Pour over the sauce, top with the sliced mozzarella and scatter over the remaining Parmesan. Bake for 30 minutes until golden. Serve hot.

Tip
For a more refined serving option, assemble and bake the moussaka in a steel ring mould set on a baking sheet. Position on a large serving plate and remove the mould just before serving.

Best of HOME COOK

MOROCCAN LAMB BURGERS WITH MINT AÏOLI

These delicious burgers, full of flavour from the fresh mint and the gentle heat of the harissa, will transport you to the souks and medinas of north Africa. The burgers can be shaped up to a day in advance and stored in the fridge, ready to cook at a moment's notice.

Serves 4
Prep time: 15 minutes
Cook time: 20 minutes

½ onion, peeled
2 garlic cloves, peeled
100g (4oz) ready-to-eat dried
    apricots
2 tsp ground cumin
25g (1oz) fresh mint leaves
500g (1lb 2oz) minced lamb shoulder
    (15–20 per cent fat content)
50g (2oz) fresh white breadcrumbs
2 tbsp harissa paste
120g (4½oz) feta, crumbled
1 tsp sea salt
sunflower oil, for frying

For the mint aïoli
200g (7oz) good-quality mayonnaise
juice of ½ lime
2 garlic cloves, crushed
20g (¾oz) fresh mint, finely chopped
pinch of sea salt

To serve
2 Little Gem lettuces, shredded
2 tbsp pomegranate seeds (optional)
4 brioche burger buns, halved
¼ cucumber, halved and thinly sliced

1. For the mint aïoli, combine all the ingredients in a bowl, cover and set aside.

2. Preheat the oven to 200°c/180°c fan/gas 6.

3. For the burgers, put the onion, garlic, apricots, cumin and mint leaves into a food processor and pulse until coarsely ground. Transfer the mixture to a bowl and add the minced lamb, breadcrumbs, harissa, feta and salt. Combine until thoroughly mixed: the best way to do this is using your hands. Fry a teaspoon of the mixture to test the seasoning: taste and adjust with a little more salt if necessary. Divide the mixture into four and shape into burgers.

4. Heat a little oil in a large ovenproof frying pan over a medium heat. Add the burgers and fry for 3–4 minutes on each side until evenly browned. Put the pan into the oven to bake for 10–12 minutes, until the burgers are just cooked through.

5. To serve, put some of the shredded lettuce and pomegranate seeds (if using) onto the base of each burger bun. Top with a burger, some cucumber and mint aïoli and the remaining half of the bun. Serve immediately.

Best of
HOME
COOK

OX CHEEK MASSAMAN CURRY

This wonderfully fragrant and warming curry is well worth the long cooking time. If ox cheek is not available, you can use stewing beef instead.

Serves 6
Prep time: 15 minutes
Cook time: 3 hours 10 minutes

2 tbsp sunflower oil

2 × 400ml tins coconut milk

100g (4oz) massaman curry paste (available in good supermarkets)

1 large or 2 smaller ox cheeks, or stewing beef, 750g (1lb 10oz) total weight, cut into bite-sized pieces

3 tbsp smooth peanut butter

150ml (¼ pint) chicken stock

250g (9oz) baby new potatoes, halved (no need to peel)

1 red onion, thickly sliced

1 fresh red chilli, de-seeded and sliced

4 fresh Kaffir lime leaves

1 cinnamon stick

3 cardamom pods

2 tbsp tamarind paste

2 tbsp palm sugar or soft brown sugar

1 tbsp fish sauce

2 limes: juice of one and the other cut into wedges

3 tbsp chopped roasted peanuts

small handful of Thai basil leaves

cooked rice, to serve

1. Preheat the oven to 160°C/140°C fan/gas 3.

2. Heat the oil in a large flameproof casserole dish (with a lid) over a medium–high heat. Once hot, add four tablespoons of the coconut milk and all the curry paste. Fry for 2–4 minutes, stirring frequently, until aromatic. Add the ox cheek or beef and fry for another 4 minutes, stirring frequently until the meat is browned on all sides. Add the remaining coconut milk, the peanut butter, stock, potatoes, onions, most of the chilli, the lime leaves, cinnamon stick, cardamom, tamarind, sugar, fish sauce and lime juice. Boil for 2 minutes, then remove from the heat.

3. Cover the dish with the lid and transfer to the oven to cook for 2½–3 hours, until the meat is meltingly tender.

4. Taste and, if necessary, adjust the seasoning with more fish sauce (or salt if you prefer) and lime juice.

5. Serve with the remaining sliced chilli, the peanuts and Thai basil scattered over and the rice and lime wedges on the side.

Best of
HOME
COOK

BEEF SHIN & OYSTER PIE

It does take a few hours to cook beef shin to get it perfectly tender; however, it is hands-off time, so you can be getting on with something else. Here, a marrow bone is cooked into the pie, providing extra flavour. It is optional, though, and the pie is just as delicious without.

Serves 4
Prep time: 15 minutes
Cook time: 3¾–4¼ hours

600g (1lb 5oz) beef shin
2 tbsp sunflower oil
1 carrot, finely diced
1 onion, finely chopped
4 garlic cloves, crushed
1 tbsp plain flour
500ml (17fl oz) porter beer
400ml (14fl oz) beef stock
3 bay leaves
4 thyme sprigs, plus extra leaves
    to scatter
1 marrow bone, 6–8cm (2½–3in)
    long (optional)
8 fresh oysters, shucked (optional)
375g (13oz) ready-rolled puff pastry
1 egg, beaten
sea salt and black pepper

1. Cut the beef shin into bite-sized pieces. Heat the oil in a large heavy-based pan (with a tight-fitting lid) over a medium–high heat. Add the beef in batches and brown on all sides for 4–6 minutes. Remove to a bowl.

2. Add the carrot and onion to the pan and sauté over a medium heat for 6–8 minutes until beginning to soften. Add the garlic and cook for 2–3 minutes until aromatic. Next, add the browned beef and the flour and stir to combine. Finally, add the beer, stock, bay leaves, thyme sprigs, one teaspoon of salt and a good grinding of black pepper. Bring to the boil, reduce the heat to very low, cover with the lid and simmer gently for 3–3½ hours, by which time the beef shin should be meltingly tender and the sauce thick and viscous.

3. Alternatively, you can cook the beef in a pressure cooker on high pressure for 50–60 minutes until tender, then simmer on the hob for a few minutes to reduce the sauce.

4. Preheat the oven to 200°C/180°C fan/gas 6.

5. Sit the marrow bone (if using) upright in a 1.5 litre (2½ pint) pie dish. Spoon in the beef and sauce and lay the oysters on top, if you are using them. Place the puff pastry sheet on top, making a hole to accommodate the marrow bone, and press around the edge of the pastry to seal it to the dish, then trim the edge using a sharp knife. Brush the pastry with beaten egg and season with a little salt, pepper and a few more thyme leaves.

6. Bake for 30–35 minutes until the pastry is risen, crisp and golden. Serve immediately.

Best of
HOME
COOK

BEEF, PRUNE & ALE STEW

The prunes here provide a delicious sweetness that works very well with the ale. This tastes even better the day after you have made it: let it cool completely, refrigerate overnight and reheat just before serving. Serve with crusty bread to mop up the juices.

Serves 4–6
Prep time: 15 minutes
Cook time: 1¾ hours

4 tbsp olive oil
650g (1lb 7oz) beef shoulder or
    stewing beef, cut into chunks
2 onions, roughly chopped
1 tsp dried chilli flakes
3 garlic cloves, crushed
2 tbsp cornflour
500ml (17fl oz) beef stock
400g (14oz) baby new potatoes,
    peeled and halved
300ml (½ pint) golden ale
120g (4½oz) soft prunes, stoned
small handful of parsley leaves,
    roughly chopped
sea salt and black pepper
crusty bread, to serve

1. Heat two tablespoons of the olive oil in a large, deep, flameproof casserole dish (with a lid) over a high heat. Once hot, brown the beef in batches on all sides for 4–6 minutes. Season with salt and pepper, remove from the pan and set aside.

2. Add the remaining olive oil, the onions and chilli flakes and sauté over a medium–high heat for 5 minutes until the onions are beginning to soften. Add the garlic and fry for 2 minutes until aromatic.

3. In a bowl, whisk together the cornflour and a few tablespoons of the stock until completely smooth. Add this to the pan, along with the remaining stock, the browned beef, new potatoes and ale. Season with one teaspoon of salt and a large pinch of pepper. Bring to the boil, then reduce the heat and simmer gently for 70–80 minutes until the meat is tender and the potatoes are soft.

4. Add the prunes to the casserole and simmer for 10 minutes, then turn off the heat and stir through most of the parsley. Taste and adjust the seasoning if necessary. Scatter over the remaining parsley and serve with crusty bread.

BEEF WELLINGTON

This classic dish of beef wrapped in mushroom paste, Parma ham and puff pastry is a showstopper for any celebratory meal, and is well worth the effort. Photographed overleaf.

Serves 6

Prep time: 30 minutes, plus cooling
    and 50 minutes chilling
Cook time: 1 hour, plus resting

25–30g (about 1oz) dried porcini
    mushrooms, soaked in boiling
    water for 20 minutes
450g (1lb) mixed fresh mushrooms
50g (2oz) unsalted butter
1 tbsp fresh thyme leaves
2 tbsp olive oil
1 fillet of beef, about 800g (1¾lb)
2 tbsp English mustard
10–12 thin slices of Parma ham
plain flour, for dusting
500g (1lb 2oz) good-quality puff
    pastry
2 egg yolks, beaten
sea salt and black pepper

Best of
HOME
COOK

1. Drain the soaked porcini mushrooms through a sieve into a bowl, squeezing out as much liquid as possible. Keep the liquid to use as stock, if you wish.

2. Put the porcini and fresh mushrooms into a food processor and blitz for a minute or so to form a paste. Heat the butter in a non-stick frying pan over a medium heat. Add the mushroom paste and thyme and fry for 15 minutes, stirring frequently, until all the liquid has evaporated and the mushrooms are quite dry. Remove to a plate and leave to cool.

3. Heat the olive oil in a large pan over a high heat. Season the beef fillet with salt and pepper and, when the oil is very hot, add the beef and sear on all sides: this should take no more than about 3 minutes. Remove to a plate and leave to cool completely. Brush the mustard all over the beef fillet.

4. Place a large piece of clingfilm on your work surface (you may need two pieces) and lay the Parma ham on top in two neat, slightly overlapping, rows, so you have a rectangular layer of ham roughly the width of your beef, that will fit around the beef when rolled up. Evenly spread the cooled mushroom paste on top. Position the beef along one short edge of the ham, then use the clingfilm to help you tightly wrap the mushroom and ham around the beef, forming a neat log shape. Twist the clingfilm at either end to make sure it is well compacted. Place in the freezer for 30 minutes to firm up.

5. Dust your work surface lightly with flour and roll out the pastry into a rectangular shape about 3mm (⅛in) thick and large enough to fully enclose the beef. Brush the pastry with egg yolk.

Take the clingfilm off the beef and position the beef along one short edge of the pastry, the one closest to you. Gently roll the beef away from you, wrapping the pastry around as you go and folding in the open ends, ensuring it is smooth with no air pockets. Trim off any excess pastry and seal the pastry very well along all seams. Place the beef seam side down on a board and brush with egg yolk. Transfer to the freezer for another 20 minutes to rest.

6. Put a baking sheet into the oven and preheat to 220°C/ 200°C fan/gas 7.

7. Remove the beef from the freezer and lightly score the pastry in a pattern: a line down the centre with diagonal lines coming off each side is traditional. Brush the pastry again with any remaining egg yolk. Sprinkle over a little sea salt.

8. Carefully transfer the beef to the preheated baking sheet and bake for 40 minutes until golden brown. You may think this high heat will overcook the beef, but as it was rested in the freezer it will take a bit of time to come up to temperature. Forty minutes at this temperature will yield a rare beef Wellington. If you prefer it medium, add another 5 minutes. If you have a meat thermometer, an internal temperature of 43°C is rare, and 49°C is medium.

9. Remove and leave to rest for 15 minutes, then transfer to a serving dish, slice and serve.

FISH

FISH BUTTIES

Deliciously crisp, breaded fish is very easy to make – have the tartare sauce, salad and bread rolls ready so you can assemble them while still hot from the pan.

Serves 4
Prep time: 15 minutes
Cook time: 15 minutes

50g (2oz) plain flour
2 tsp smoked paprika
2 eggs, beaten
200g (7oz) fresh or
    dried breadcrumbs
4 cod, haddock or halibut fillets,
    total weight about 600g (1lb 5oz),
    skin removed, cut into 12 fingers
sunflower oil for frying
large handful of rocket or
    lamb's lettuce
4 baps or bread rolls, halved
sea salt and black pepper

For the tartare sauce
200g (7oz) mayonnaise
2 tbsp cornichons, finely chopped
1 tbsp capers, chopped
2 spring onions, finely chopped
2 tsp Dijon mustard
1 tbsp fresh lemon juice

1. To make the tartare sauce, mix everything together in a bowl and set aside.

2. In a bowl, combine the flour and smoked paprika with one teaspoon of salt and plenty of freshly ground black pepper. Put the eggs in a shallow dish and the breadcrumbs in another. Coat each fish finger in the seasoned flour, then in the beaten egg and finally roll in the breadcrumbs until evenly covered.

3. Fill a large deep heavy-based pan with oil to a depth of 1cm (½in) and place over a medium–high heat. Test the oil is hot enough by dropping in a small piece of bread: it should brown in 40–50 seconds. When hot, fry the fish fingers in batches for 2–3 minutes on each side until golden and crisp. Remove, sprinkle with sea salt, drain on kitchen paper and keep warm while you cook the remaining fish fingers.

4. Put some rocket or lamb's lettuce and a large dollop of the tartare sauce onto the base of each bap or bread roll. Top with three fish fingers and the remaining half of the bap or roll and serve immediately.

BUTTER-POACHED HALIBUT WITH GIROLLES, SAMPHIRE & LEMON AÏOLI

In this indulgent dish, the fish is poached in melted butter infused with herbs and aromatics, resulting in beautifully tender and moist halibut.

Serves 4
Prep time: 10 minutes
Cook time: 30 minutes

250g (9oz) unsalted butter,
    plus 3 tbsp
1 lemon: grated zest and 2 tbsp juice
1 tbsp capers
small handful of dill fronds,
    roughly chopped
2 bay leaves
4 × 120–150g (4½–5oz) halibut fillets,
    skin on
60g (2½oz) samphire
400g (14oz) chanterelle (girolle) or
    shiitake mushrooms, halved
1 tbsp fresh thyme leaves
sea salt and black pepper

For the lemon aïoli
150g (5oz) good-quality mayonnaise
grated zest of 1 lemon and juice of
    ½ lemon
1 garlic clove, crushed
pinch of sea salt

1. For the lemon aïoli, combine all the ingredients in a bowl, cover and set aside.

2. Preheat the oven to 150°C/130°C fan/gas 2. Line a small roasting tin with a double layer of foil or baking parchment, leaving enough overhanging to fully enclose the fish.

3. Put the 250g of butter into a small pan, together with the lemon zest and juice, capers, dill and bay leaves, and heat through over a medium–low heat until melted. Season the halibut on both sides with salt and pepper and place in the lined tin.

4. Once the butter has melted, pour over the halibut and turn to coat the fish in the butter, then lift up the overhanging foil and enclose the fish to create a parcel. Bake for 15 minutes, then remove from the oven but do not open the foil for 5 minutes.

5. Meanwhile, put the samphire in a bowl, boil a kettle of water and pour over the samphire; leave to sit for 5 minutes, then drain. Put the remaining three tablespoons of butter into a large pan over a high heat. Once the butter is foaming, add the mushrooms, thyme and blanched samphire and fry for 6–8 minutes until the mushrooms are golden.

6. Plate up the halibut fillets with the mushrooms and samphire tumbling off the fish and the lemon aïoli on the side.

Tip
If halibut is not available, you could use cod or haddock instead.

BAKED TROUT WITH POTATO, TOMATO & SAFFRON

Trout is a delicious fish, with a more delicate flavour than salmon, and perfect for roasting whole. Saffron imparts a fragrant earthy flavour, and gives a beautiful golden-yellow hue to everything it touches, including – if you are not careful – your kitchen worktop!

Serves 4
Prep time: 15 minutes
Cook time: 55 minutes

1kg (2lb 3oz) floury potatoes (such as Maris Piper), peeled
5 tbsp olive oil
6 garlic cloves, sliced
500g (1lb 2oz) cherry tomatoes, halved
2 rosemary sprigs, leaves removed and chopped
large pinch of saffron threads
2 trout, cleaned, gutted and scaled (ask your fishmonger to prepare it for you)
small handful of flat-leaf parsley leaves, chopped
sea salt and black pepper

1. Preheat the oven to 200°C/180°C fan/gas 6.

2. Cut the potatoes into slices 1cm (½in) thick. Transfer to a large roasting tin with four tablespoons of the olive oil, the garlic, cherry tomatoes, rosemary, saffron, three-quarters of a teaspoon of salt and a large pinch of black pepper. Gently combine everything together until evenly mixed. Bake for 40 minutes.

3. Meanwhile, coat the trout with the remaining tablespoon of olive oil and season with salt and pepper, both inside and out. Place the fish on top of the potatoes and bake for a further 12–15 minutes, until the fish is just cooked through and the potatoes are tender.

4. Serve in the roasting tin, or fillet the fish and plate up individually, with the potatoes, tomatoes and the parsley scattered over.

PAN-FRIED COD WITH NEW POTATOES, BROCCOLI & PRAWN BISQUE SAUCE

If you're short of time, the cod can be served without the prawn bisque sauce. However, the sauce can be made in advance, cooled and stored in the freezer, so it is a good recipe to double up on.

Best of HOME COOK

Serves 4
Prep time: 5–10 minutes,
    plus cooling
Cook time: 20 minutes, plus
    20 minutes for the sauce

600g (1lb 5oz) new potatoes, halved
300g (10½oz) tenderstem broccoli
4 tbsp salted butter
small handful of chives, finely
    chopped, plus extra to serve
4 × 120g (4½oz) cod loins, skin on
3 tbsp olive oil
2 tbsp fresh lemon juice
sea salt and black pepper

For the prawn bisque sauce (optional)
1 tbsp unsalted butter
150g (5oz) raw tiger prawns, shell on
½ onion, finely chopped
½ carrot, finely chopped
1 bay leaf
1 tbsp cognac or brandy
50g (2oz) cherry tomatoes, halved
2 tbsp dry white wine
1 tarragon sprig
250ml (9fl oz) fish stock
100ml (3½fl oz) double cream
1 tsp fresh lemon juice
sea salt and black pepper

1. To make the sauce, melt the butter in a frying pan over a medium–high heat. Add the prawns and fry for 4–5 minutes, turning now and again, until pink and cooked through. Add the onion, carrot, bay leaf and cognac or brandy and bring to the boil, then immediately add the tomatoes, wine, tarragon, fish stock and cream. Bring to the boil, reduce the heat slightly and simmer for 10 minutes until thick and creamy.

2. Leave to cool for 10 minutes, then purée using a blender or food processor until almost smooth. Strain through a fine sieve into a bowl, pressing through as much liquid as possible. Season to taste with the lemon juice, salt and pepper and set aside.

3. Bring a large pan of salted water to the boil and put the potatoes in to cook for 15 minutes. Add the broccoli and cook for another 3–4 minutes, until a sharp knife glides into the centre of a potato without resistance and the broccoli is tender but not soft. Drain the vegetables, return to the pan and toss with half the butter and the chives and season with a little salt and pepper.

4. Meanwhile, season the cod on both sides with salt and pepper. Heat the oil in a frying pan over a medium heat. Add the cod, skin side down, and fry for 3–4 minutes until the skin is crisp. Turn the fish over, add the remaining butter and the lemon juice and fry for another 1–2 minutes until cooked through.

5. Serve the fish with the potatoes and broccoli and some chives scattered over. If you are serving this with the sauce, gently reheat the sauce in a small pan, then pour about three tablespoons of sauce into each wide, shallow bowl. Place the potato, broccoli and cod on top and serve with some chives scattered over.

CRAB PITHIVIER

This classic French puff-pastry pie, reimagined with a tasty crab filling, can be made in advance and frozen uncooked; thaw before cooking.

Serves 8
Prep time: 20 minutes,
    plus cooling and chilling
Cook time: 55 minutes

200g (7oz) fresh white and
    brown crab meat
2 tsp capers, rinsed
1 tsp Dijon mustard
500g (1lb 2oz) puff pastry
1 egg, beaten

For the béchamel sauce
2 tbsp unsalted butter
30g (1oz) plain flour, plus extra
    for dusting
300ml (½ pint) whole milk
sea salt and black pepper

1. First, make the béchamel sauce: melt the butter in a pan over a medium–low heat, add the flour, stir to combine and cook for 2 minutes, stirring all the time. Whisk in the milk, a little at a time, until you have a smooth sauce. Continue cooking for 10 minutes over a low heat, stirring all the time, until the sauce is thick and creamy. Season to taste with salt and pepper and leave to cool completely.

2. Once the béchamel sauce is cool, weigh out 100g (4oz) and combine with the crab meat, capers and mustard. Season to taste with a little salt and pepper, bearing in mind the capers are already salty. Keep the remaining béchamel covered in the fridge; you can use it to make lasagne or another dish.

3. Preheat the oven to 200°C/180°C fan/gas 6. Line a baking sheet with baking parchment.

4. Divide the pastry in half. Roll out both pieces to a thickness of about 3mm (⅛in) on a worktop dusted in flour. Cut out a 23cm (9in) disc from each piece of pastry (use the base of a 23cm round cake tin as a guide). Transfer the pastry discs to a plate or chopping board and place in the freezer for 15 minutes to rest.

5. Remove one disc of pastry from the freezer and place on the lined baking sheet. Spoon the crab mixture on top in a shallow dome shape, leaving a 1cm (½in) border around the edge. Brush the edge of the pastry with the beaten egg. Remove the second disc of pastry from the freezer and, using the tip of a very sharp knife, cut out a 1cm (½in) circle in the centre of the disc and remove. Lightly score curved lines into the pastry, emanating from the central hole, taking great care not to cut all the way through. Position this disc on top of the filling and seal the pastry edges together, using your fingers and crimping the edge with the back of a knife as you go. Brush the top of the pastry with beaten egg and bake for 35–45 minutes until deep golden brown, risen and crisp. Leave to cool for 5 minutes, then serve.

GINGER TERIYAKI TROUT

Making your own teriyaki sauce is simple, quick and delicious.
A red or yellow pepper makes a good substitute for the carrot
in the stir-fried vegetables, if desired.

Serves 2
Prep time: 5 minutes,
    plus 1 hour (minimum)
    marinating
Cook time: 10 minutes

2 tbsp soy sauce, plus 2 tsp
1 tbsp runny honey
grated zest and juice of 1 lime
2cm (¾in) piece of fresh root ginger,
    peeled and very thinly sliced
1 tsp caster sugar
2 trout fillets, skin on
3 tbsp sunflower oil
250g (9oz) mangetout
1 carrot, cut into matchsticks
1 tsp roasted sesame seed oil
2 spring onions, finely sliced

1. In a bowl, combine two tablespoons of the soy sauce with the honey, lime zest and juice, ginger and sugar. Add the trout fillets and turn to coat. Leave to marinate in the refrigerator for at least 1 hour, or overnight.

2. For the vegetables, heat two tablespoons of the sunflower oil in a frying pan over a high heat. Once hot, add the mangetout and carrot and stir-fry for 3–4 minutes until beginning to soften. Remove and toss with the remaining two teaspoons of soy sauce and the sesame seed oil. Keep warm while you cook the fish.

3. Wipe out the pan and return to the heat. Pour in the marinade liquid and simmer for 3 minutes to reduce. Remove to a bowl. Add the remaining sunflower oil and, once hot, add the trout, skin side down, and fry for 3 minutes until the skin is golden and crisp. Turn and fry the other side for 1–2 minutes until just cooked through.

4. Serve the fish with the vegetables, the reduced marinade on the side and the spring onions scattered over.

Best of
HOME
COOK

FISH PIE

This classic fish pie is the ultimate comfort food, creamy and warming and easy to make.

Serves 4–6
Prep time: 20 minutes
Cook time: 50 minutes

900g (2lb) floury potatoes
    (such as Maris Piper), peeled
    and quartered
120g (4½oz) unsalted butter
300ml (½ pint) milk
½ onion, finely chopped
50g (2oz) plain flour
200ml (7fl oz) fish or chicken stock
large handful of flat-leaf parsley
    leaves, finely chopped,
    plus extra to serve
2½ tsp Dijon mustard
200g (7oz) white fish fillet, such as
    cod or haddock, skinned and cut
    into bite-sized pieces
200g (7oz) salmon fillet, skinned and
    cut into bite-sized pieces
400g (14oz) smoked white fish fillet,
    cut into bite-sized pieces
100g (4oz) raw peeled prawns
small handful of freshly grated
    Cheddar
sea salt and black pepper

1. Preheat the oven to 200°c/180°c fan/gas 6.

2. Put the potatoes into a large pot, cover with water and bring to the boil. Reduce the heat and simmer for 15–20 minutes until tender. Drain the potatoes, then mash until smooth with 75g (3oz) of the butter and 100ml (3½fl oz) of the milk. Season to taste with salt and pepper. Set aside.

3. While the potatoes are cooking, put 25g (1oz) of the remaining butter into a pan with the onion and sauté over a medium heat for 8 minutes until softened. Remove to a plate.

4. Add the remaining butter to the pan and, once melted, add the flour and stir to combine. Cook for 2 minutes, stirring all the time. Add the remaining milk a little at a time, stirring constantly, until you have a smooth sauce. Stir in the stock and bring to the boil, then reduce the heat and simmer for 5–7 minutes, stirring frequently, until thickened. Stir in the parsley, mustard and fried onion and season to taste with salt and pepper.

5. Stir the fish and prawns into the sauce and transfer to a large baking dish. Top with the mashed potato and the grated cheese and bake for 25–30 minutes until golden and bubbling. Scatter over a little parsley and serve immediately.

CRAB CUSTARD TART

This is a really elegant tart, equally good served warm
from the oven or at room temperature.

Serves 8
Prep time: 20 minutes, plus chilling
    and cooling
Cook time: 50 minutes

375g (13oz) ready-rolled puff pastry
300g (10½oz) fresh white and
    brown crab meat
1 lemon: grated zest and 1 tbsp juice
4 spring onions, finely sliced
small handful of dill fronds, roughly
    chopped, plus extra to serve
small handful of coriander leaves,
    roughly chopped, plus extra
    to serve
3 eggs
200ml (7fl oz) double cream
sea salt and black pepper

1. Preheat the oven to 200°c/180°c fan/gas 6.

2. Line a 24cm (9½in) round fluted loose-bottomed tart tin
with the puff pastry and trim the edges with a sharp knife. Cover
and chill for 15 minutes in the fridge or 5 minutes in the freezer.
Prick the base of the pastry all over with a fork, line with baking
parchment, fill with baking beans and blind bake for 20 minutes.
Remove the paper and beans and bake for a further 5 minutes
until the pastry is golden. The centre of the pastry may rise: if
this happens, gently press it back down when you take it out of
the oven.

3. Meanwhile, squeeze any excess liquid out of the crab meat.
Add the crab to a bowl, together with the lemon zest and juice
and most of the spring onions, dill and coriander. Season to taste
with salt and pepper.

4. In another bowl, beat together the eggs and cream with the
remaining chopped herbs and spring onions. Season with a
quarter of a teaspoon of salt and some pepper. Pour this into the
baked pastry case, then add the crab mixture, so it is still visible in
places above the egg and cream mixture. Bake for 20–25 minutes
until golden and set.

5. Remove from the oven and leave to cool for 10 minutes, then
serve with a few dill fronds and coriander leaves scattered over.

Tip
If you are not keen on dill, parsley also works well with
the coriander.

Best of
HOME
COOK

PAN-FRIED SPICY MACKEREL

Mackerel is a tasty and inexpensive fish, but it is important to use very fresh mackerel. With the mildly spiced sauce, these fillets are delicious served with Golden Bombay Potatoes (page 71).

Serves 4
Prep time: 5 minutes
Cook time: 10–15 minutes

½ onion, peeled
2 tomatoes
1 tsp ground cumin
1 tsp ground coriander
2 tbsp olive oil
8 mackerel fillets, skin on
2 tsp fresh lemon juice
sea salt and black pepper

1. Put the onion, tomatoes, cumin, coriander, one tablespoon of the oil and a large pinch of salt and pepper into a food processor and blitz until smooth. Transfer to a pan, place over a medium heat and cook for 6 minutes, stirring frequently, to cook off the onion and reduce the sauce slightly. Set aside.

2. Heat the remaining oil in a large non-stick frying pan over a medium–high heat. Season the mackerel fillets on both sides with salt and pepper, then add to the hot pan, skin side down. Fry for 3 minutes, without moving the fillets, until the skin is crispy and golden brown. Flip over and cook for another 1–2 minutes, just until the fish is cooked through. Add the lemon juice and let it sizzle for a few seconds. Remove from the pan and serve immediately, with the sauce.

Best of
HOME
COOK

BAKING

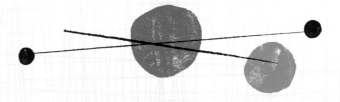

CRUMPETS

Crumpets are undoubtedly more delicious when freshly made, warm from the pan, with lashings of salted butter and whatever else you wish to top them with. The yeasted batter means that they take a little time to make, so this recipe is good for a leisurely weekend morning.

Makes about 10 crumpets
Prep time: 20 minutes,
    plus 1–1½ hours rising
Cook time: 10–12 minutes per batch
VEGETARIAN

vegetable oil, for greasing
    and cooking
250ml (9fl oz) whole milk
100ml (3½fl oz) warm water
1 tsp caster sugar
2 × 7g sachets fast-action dried yeast
250g (9oz) strong white bread flour
1 tsp fine sea salt
½ tsp bicarbonate of soda
salted butter and jam, to serve

1. You will need four metal rings, 8–10cm (3–4in) in diameter, liberally greased on the inside with vegetable oil.

2. Warm the milk in a pan over a low heat. Stir in the warm water, sugar and yeast and leave in a warm place for about 10 minutes or until frothy.

3. Sift the flour, salt and bicarbonate of soda into a bowl. Make a well in the centre and pour in the milk and yeast mixture. Whisk together until smooth. Cover and set aside in a warm place for 1–1½ hours, until the surface is covered with tiny bubbles.

4. Place a heavy-based non-stick pan over a medium–low heat. Grease with a little oil and set the metal rings in the pan. Once hot, pour three tablespoons of batter into each ring: this may look like a small amount, but the crumpets will rise, so do not overfill the metal rings. Cook for 7–10 minutes until the base is golden, the surface is almost dry and the bubbles have popped, leaving lots of little holes. This may take a little more or less time, depending on your heat source and pan: the temperature should be sufficiently low so as not to burn the base before the top is mostly dry. Carefully remove the metal rings, with the aid of a knife if necessary, then flip over the crumpets and cook for another minute or two until golden. Remove and keep warm while you cook the remaining batter in the same way.

5. Serve while still warm, with butter and jam, or leave them to cool and reheat in the pan for a minute or two on each side when ready to serve.

DATE & PEANUT BUTTER FLAPJACKS

The classic flapjack gets a delicious twist with peanut butter and dates. If you have a nut allergy, you can replace the peanut butter with tahini (made from sesame seeds) or leave it out completely and increase the butter by 25g (1oz).

Makes 12 flapjacks
Prep time: 10 minutes, plus cooling
Cook time: 30–35 minutes
VEGETARIAN

320g (11oz) unsalted butter, plus
    extra for greasing
100g (4oz) golden caster sugar
100g (4oz) crunchy peanut butter
50g (2oz) golden syrup
100g (4oz) dates, pitted and chopped
pinch of sea salt
250g (9oz) jumbo oats
250g (9oz) quick-cook oats

1. Preheat the oven to 180°C/160°C fan/gas 4. Butter a 24 × 15cm (9½ × 6in) tray bake or roasting tin and line with baking parchment.

2. Put the butter, sugar, peanut butter, golden syrup and dates into a large pan and place over a medium heat. Simmer gently until the sugar has completely dissolved and the mixture is bubbling. Stir in the salt. Remove the pan from the heat, tip in the oats and stir until very well combined.

3. Transfer the mixture into the prepared tin and press flat. Bake for 30–35 minutes until deep golden brown. Remove from the oven and leave to cool for 10 minutes, then cut the flapjacks into 12 squares and leave in the tin to cool completely. Remove the flapjack slab from the tin and break the squares apart. Store in an airtight container for up to a week.

ECCLES CAKES

This dense, fruit-filled pastry, hailing from the town of Eccles in northern England, is a classic teatime, or anytime, treat. More akin to a mince pie than a cake, it keeps well once cooled, and is also delicious with a slice of Lancashire cheese.

Makes 12 pastries
Prep time: 30 minutes
Cook time: 20–25 minutes
VEGETARIAN

25g (1oz) salted butter, at room temperature
150g (5oz) currants
40g (1½oz) chopped mixed peel
50g (2oz) light muscovado sugar
1 tbsp brandy
½ tsp ground cinnamon
½ tsp mixed spice
grated zest of 1 orange
plain flour, for dusting
500g (1lb 2oz) ready-rolled puff pastry
1 egg white
3 tbsp demerara sugar, for sprinkling
Lancashire cheese, to serve

1. Preheat the oven to 200°C/180°C fan/gas 6. Line two baking sheets with baking parchment.

2. Put the butter, currants, mixed peel, muscovado sugar, brandy, cinnamon, mixed spice and orange zest into a large bowl and mix together until thoroughly combined. Set aside.

3. Spread out the pastry on a worktop dusted with flour and use a 10cm (4in) round pastry cutter to punch out 12 discs of puff pastry. Divide the dried fruit mixture between the 12 discs, then brush the edges with a little water. One at a time, take the outer edge of each disc of pastry and bring it together at the top, squeezing it tightly to seal in the filling. Gently flatten the pastry between the palms of your hands, so you are left with a patty with the filling inside.

4. Place the Eccles cakes onto the lined baking sheets, smooth side facing up. Brush with egg white and sprinkle with the demerara sugar. Make three short, shallow cuts on the top of each cake to allow steam to escape.

5. Bake for 20–25 minutes until deep golden brown and crisp, with a caramelised crust. Leave to cool on a wire rack before serving.

WINTER-SPICED PLUM PLAIT

This beautiful puff pastry plait is perfect for the winter months when you want something warming and indulgent, yet light and crisp. Photographed overleaf.

Serves 4–6
Prep time: 25 minutes, plus cooling
Cook time: 1 hour 5 minutes
VEGETARIAN

500g (1lb 2oz) plums, stoned and
    chopped into small pieces
½ apple, cored and finely chopped
400ml (14fl oz) red wine (e.g. Merlot)
1 tsp ground nutmeg
1 cinnamon stick
2 strips of orange zest
5 tbsp muscovado sugar
375g (13oz) ready-rolled puff pastry
1 egg, beaten
2 tsp demerara sugar
1 tbsp raw shelled pistachio nuts,
    roughly chopped
ice cream or whipped cream, to serve

For the crème pâtissière
150ml (¼ pint) milk
100ml (3½fl oz) double cream
1 vanilla pod, slit lengthways and
    seeds scraped out
50g (2oz) caster sugar
3 egg yolks
1½ tsp cornflour, sifted
1 tsp plain flour, sifted
1 tbsp icing sugar, plus extra to serve

1. Put the plums, apple, wine, nutmeg, cinnamon stick, orange zest and muscovado sugar into a pan and bring to the boil. Immediately reduce the heat and simmer for 15 minutes. Strain the cooking liquid into a bowl and keep for making mulled wine. Discard the cinnamon stick and orange zest. Leave the plums to cool.

2. For the crème pâtissière, put the milk and cream into a heavy-based pan and place over a high heat. Add the vanilla pod and seeds. Bring to the boil and immediately reduce the heat and simmer for 3 minutes. Turn off the heat and discard the vanilla pod.

3. Using an electric whisk or a stand mixer, whisk the caster sugar and egg yolks together until pale and creamy; this may take 5 minutes or more. Whisk in the flours until fully incorporated.

4. With the whisk running, pour half the warm milk and cream into the egg and sugar mixture and whisk until combined. Now pour this back into the pan of warm milk and cream. Place over a medium heat and begin whisking continuously. After 1–2 minutes it will thicken and rise; when this happens, reduce the heat to low and keep whisking quickly for another 2 minutes until you have a very thick crème pâtissière.

5. Transfer the crème pâtissière to a clean baking sheet, smooth out the mixture and dust with the icing sugar to prevent a skin forming. Set aside to cool, then place in the freezer for 10 minutes until ice cold.

6. Put a baking sheet into the oven and preheat to 200°C/ 180°C fan/gas 6.

7. Lay a large sheet of baking parchment on your work surface. Place the rectangular sheet of puff pastry on top and score the pastry lengthways into three equal strips, ensuring you do not cut all the way through. Slice the outer strips of pastry on either side crossways into strips 2cm (¾in) wide, leaving the central section of pastry whole.

8. Spread the chilled crème pâtissière over the central section of pastry, then spread the plums on top. Fold the strips of pastry from each side over the plums, interweaving them as you go. Brush the pastry with the beaten egg and sprinkle over the demerara sugar.

9. Remove the baking sheet from the oven and carefully slide the baking parchment and pastry onto the hot sheet. Bake for 25 minutes. Scatter over the pistachios and bake for a further 10–15 minutes until the pastry is crisp and deep golden brown.

10. Leave to cool slightly, then dust with icing sugar and serve with ice cream or whipped cream.

GINGERBREAD

This recipe comes from the north of England, where it is known as parkin. It is rich and moist, with a delicious warmth from the ground ginger. Perfect for afternoon tea, it keeps very well and can be made up to three weeks in advance.

Makes 15 pieces
Prep time: 15 minutes, plus cooling
Cook time: 1¼ hours
VEGETARIAN

120g (4½oz) black treacle
100g (4oz) golden syrup
200g (7oz) unsalted butter, plus extra
    for greasing
150g (5oz) soft dark brown sugar
200g (7oz) plain flour
200g (7oz) medium oatmeal
1 tbsp ground ginger
1½ tsp bicarbonate of soda
¼ tsp sea salt
1 egg, beaten
3 tbsp milk

1. Preheat the oven to 160°C/140°C fan/gas 3. Butter a 24 × 18cm (9½ × 7in) baking tin and line the base with baking parchment.

2. Gently melt the treacle, golden syrup, butter and sugar in a pan over a low heat, taking care not to let it boil. Once the sugar has dissolved, remove the pan from the heat.

3. Put the flour, oatmeal, ginger, bicarbonate of soda and salt into a bowl. Mix in the treacle and butter mixture, followed by the egg and milk, until evenly combined.

4. Pour the mixture into the prepared tin and bake for 60–70 minutes until just firm to the touch. Leave to cool in the tin, then turn out, cut into 15 squares and serve immediately, or wrap in baking parchment and foil and store in an airtight container for up to three weeks. The consistency will become fudgier and more dense as the days go by.

CARROT CAKE

This gorgeous and moist carrot cake is perfect for any tea party or birthday – or for no other reason than to enjoy a delicious slice of home-made cake one afternoon.

Serves 10
Prep time: 25 minutes, plus cooling
Cook time: 20–25 minutes
VEGETARIAN

4 eggs
225g (8oz) light muscovado sugar
250ml (9fl oz) sunflower oil
300g (10½oz) plain flour
2 tsp baking powder
200g (7oz) carrots, coarsely grated
50g (2oz) walnuts, coarsely chopped
1 tbsp finely chopped stem ginger
1½ tsp ground cinnamon
1½ tsp mixed spice
1 tsp ground ginger
grated zest of 1 orange
2 tsp orange extract
50g (2oz) pecan halves

For the icing
100g (4oz) unsalted butter, at room
    temperature
200g (7oz) icing sugar, sifted
200g (7oz) full-fat cream cheese
100g (4oz) mascarpone cheese
2 oranges: finely grated zest of one,
    pared zest of the other
2 tbsp triple sec (optional)

1. Preheat the oven to 180°C/160°C fan/gas 4. Grease two 20cm (8in) round cake tins and line the bases with baking parchment.

2. Using an electric whisk or stand mixer with whisk attachment, whisk the eggs and sugar together on high speed for 7 minutes until pale and creamy. Stir in the oil and fold in the flour, baking powder, carrots, chopped nuts, the stem ginger, cinnamon, mixed spice, ground ginger, orange zest and orange extract.

3. Divide between the prepared cake tins and bake for 20–25 minutes, until a skewer comes out clean. Leave to cool in the tins for 10 minutes, then turn out onto a wire rack and leave to cool completely.

4. While the cake is cooling, make the icing. Put the butter and icing sugar into a bowl and whisk to combine. Stir in the cream cheese, mascarpone, finely grated orange zest and the triple sec (if using). Cover and refrigerate until needed. Cut the pared zest of the second orange into thin strips and set aside.

5. Place one cake on a plate and spread with half the icing. Place the second cake on top and spread with the remaining icing. Decorate the cake with the strips of orange zest and the pecan halves.

Best of
HOME
COOK

LEMON & POPPY SEED LOAF CAKE

I have paired this teatime treat with an indulgent cream cheese frosting. You could go down a more traditional route with a simple lemon icing (see tip).

Serves 8–10
Prep time: 10 minutes, plus cooling
Cook time: 45–50 minutes
VEGETARIAN

120g (4½oz) unsalted butter,
    at room temperature, plus extra
    for greasing
175g (6oz) caster sugar
150ml (¼ pint) milk
3 eggs, beaten
2 lemons: grated zest and 2 tbsp juice
60g (2½oz) poppy seeds
1½ tsp baking powder
300g (10½oz) plain flour

For the frosting
300g (10½oz) full-fat cream cheese
grated zest of 2 lemons, plus extra
    strips of zest to decorate
1 tbsp set honey

1. Preheat the oven to 180°c/160°c fan/gas 4. Butter a 20 × 10cm (8 × 4in) loaf tin and line with baking parchment.

2. Using an electric whisk or stand mixer with whisk attachment, whisk the butter and sugar together on high speed until pale, thick and creamy. Gradually whisk in the milk, eggs, lemon zest and juice. Gently fold in the poppy seeds, baking powder and flour, just until incorporated.

3. Transfer the mixture to the prepared tin and bake for 45–50 minutes, until a skewer comes out almost clean: the cake should be slightly moist. If the top is browning too quickly, cover with foil. Leave in the tin to cool for 10 minutes, then transfer to a wire rack to cool completely.

4. Meanwhile, make the frosting. In a bowl, combine the cream cheese, lemon zest and honey and store in the fridge. Once the cake is completely cool, spread the frosting on top and scatter over a little lemon zest.

Tip
To make a simple lemon icing, sift 300g (10½oz) icing sugar into a bowl and mix until smooth with the grated zest and juice of one lemon and a knob of melted butter. When the cake is cool, spoon the icing over the top of the cake: it will run down the sides. Leave to set before slicing.

WALNUT & COFFEE SWISS ROLL

A delicious combination of coffee and walnuts in this grown-up
version of a Swiss roll, which is best enjoyed on the day of baking.

Serves 6–8
Prep time: 35 minutes, plus cooling
Cook time: 20 minutes
VEGETARIAN

160g (5½oz) walnut halves
140g (5oz) caster sugar,
    plus extra for dusting
4 eggs
140g (5oz) plain flour, plus extra
    for dusting
3 tbsp unsalted butter, melted,
    plus extra for greasing

For the filling
2 tsp instant coffee granules
2 tsp boiling water
170ml (6fl oz) double cream
25g (1oz) icing sugar, plus extra
    for dusting

1. Preheat the oven to 200°C/180°C fan/gas 6. Butter a 34 × 22cm
(13 × 8½in) Swiss roll tin and line with baking parchment.

2. Roast the walnuts in the oven for 5 minutes, until a shade
darker and aromatic. Let cool, then finely chop half the walnuts.

3. Using an electric whisk or stand mixer with whisk attachment,
whisk the sugar and eggs together until pale, thick and creamy
and at least doubled in volume. This will take 8–10 minutes.

4. Sift a few tablespoons of flour at a time into the bowl, and
very gently fold into the mixture. When all the flour has been
incorporated, gently fold in most of the chopped walnuts and
the butter. Be patient and do not knock out too much air.

5. Transfer the mixture to the prepared tin and smooth out using
the back of a spoon. Bake for 10–12 minutes until golden brown
and slightly springy to the touch. Do not leave to cool.

6. While the sponge is still warm, place a large sheet of baking
parchment on your work surface and dust liberally with caster
sugar. Supporting it with your hand, carefully invert the sponge
onto the parchment. Gently peel off the top layer of parchment.
Trim the very outer edge of the sponge with a sharp knife. Score
a line 2cm (¾in) in from the short end of the sponge closest to
you, but do not cut all the way through. Using the parchment,
tightly roll up the sponge and leave to cool, seam side down.

7. For the filling, mix the coffee and boiling water to form a paste.
In a large bowl, whisk together the cream, icing sugar and coffee
paste until soft peaks form. Cover and refrigerate until needed.

8. Gently unroll the cooled sponge. Spread the cream over the
surface, leaving a 1–2cm (½–¾in) border all round. Scatter over
the remaining chopped walnuts. Roll up the sponge again and
place on a serving plate, seam side down. Arrange the whole
walnuts on top and dust with icing sugar before serving.

MANGO & RASPBERRY CAKE

This fresh and fruity cake is full of tropical flavours. It is inspired by the mango and raspberry cake on the show, but in a simplified style for the home baker. The cake is best enjoyed within a day of baking, while the fruit and yoghurt are fresh.

Serves 8–10
Prep time: 15 minutes, plus cooling
Cook time: 40–45 minutes
VEGETARIAN

4 eggs
150g (5oz) caster sugar
grated zest of 2 lemons
60g (2½oz) desiccated coconut
175g (6oz) unsalted butter, melted
1 tsp coconut essence
4 tbsp milk
160g (5½oz) plain flour
2 tsp baking powder
1 mango, peeled and stone removed
200g (7oz) raspberries
250g (9oz) natural Greek-style or
    coconut yoghurt
5 physalis, to decorate (optional)

1. Preheat the oven to 180°c/160°c fan/gas 4. Butter a 23cm (9in) round cake tin and line the base with baking parchment.

2. Using an electric whisk or stand mixer with whisk attachment, whisk the eggs and sugar together on high speed for 5 minutes until pale and creamy. Whisk in the lemon zest, desiccated coconut, melted butter, coconut essence and milk. Sift and fold in the flour and baking powder, making sure they are thoroughly combined, then pour into the cake tin.

3. Cut half the mango into 1cm (½in) dice and scatter most of the pieces over the cake batter. Do the same with a quarter of the raspberries. Bake for 20 minutes. Take the cake out of the oven and scatter the remaining chopped mango and another quarter of the raspberries over the cake. Return to the oven and bake for another 20–25 minutes, until a skewer comes out clean. Remove from the oven and leave to cool in the tin.

4. Once completely cool, carefully transfer the cake onto a plate. Dollop the yoghurt onto the centre of the cake, so you can still see the edges. Slice the remaining half mango into thin wedges and scatter over the cake with the remaining raspberries and physalis, if using.

5. This cake is best eaten fresh, but it can be stored in an airtight container in the fridge for up to two days.

CHOCOLATE & HAZELNUT CAKE

This is a most indulgent cake, one to sit down and ruminate over, where all conversation, no matter how absorbing, must pause to give way to eating it. It pays homage to the enduring marriage of chocolate and hazelnuts, but is also good with ground almonds (see tip).

Serves 12
Prep time: 15 minutes, plus cooling
Cook time: 35–40 minutes
VEGETARIAN

150g (5oz) blanched hazelnuts
350g (12oz) dark chocolate
    (70 per cent cocoa solids),
    broken into small pieces
350g (12oz) unsalted butter, plus
    extra for greasing
60g (2½oz) cocoa powder,
    plus extra for dusting
150g (5oz) soft brown sugar
150g (5oz) caster sugar
¼ tsp sea salt
8 eggs
natural yoghurt or vanilla
    ice cream, to serve

1. Preheat the oven to 200°C/180°C fan/gas 6. Butter a 23cm (9in) round springform tin and line the base with baking parchment.

2. Roast the hazelnuts on a baking sheet in the oven for 4–6 minutes, until golden brown and aromatic. Remove and let cool completely. Turn the oven down to 160°C/140°C fan/gas 3.

3. Melt the chocolate and butter in a large heatproof bowl over a pan of barely simmering water.

4. When the hazelnuts are cool, put 100g (4oz) into a food processor and grind to a powder. Don't worry if it seems a little gritty. In a bowl, combine the ground hazelnuts and cocoa powder. Cut the remaining hazelnuts in half and set aside.

5. When the chocolate and butter have melted, remove from the heat and stir in all the sugar and the salt. One by one, whisk in the eggs, whisking very quickly and continuously until each egg is fully incorporated before adding the next one, resulting in a thick, shiny mixture. Stir in the ground hazelnuts and cocoa mixture and pour into the prepared tin.

6. Bake for 35–40 minutes, or until the cake is mostly set but with a little wobble in the centre. Leave to cool completely, then remove from the tin.

7. To serve, dust the cake with cocoa powder and place the remaining hazelnuts on top. Serve with yoghurt or ice cream.

Tip
If you feel it's too much trouble to roast and grind the hazelnuts yourself, combine 100g (4oz) ground almonds with the cocoa powder, and decorate the cake with halved or flaked almonds.

MIXED BERRY CELEBRATION CAKE

For a special occasion there is nothing like a tiered sponge cake with a rich buttercream icing and a mound of berries on top. You can decorate the cake with flowers, but it is just as beautiful without.

Serves 10–12
Prep time: 30 minutes, plus cooling
Cook time: 30–35 minutes
VEGETARIAN

200g (7oz) unsalted butter, softened, plus extra for greasing
400g (14oz) caster sugar
3 eggs, beaten
400g (14oz) plain flour
2 tsp baking powder
1 tsp bicarbonate of soda
1 tsp fine sea salt
375ml (13fl oz) milk
175g (6oz) natural Greek-style yoghurt
2 tsp vanilla extract
grated zest of 2 lemons
150g (5oz) mixed berries and edible flowers (optional), to decorate

For the icing
400g (14oz) unsalted butter, softened
550g (1¼lb) icing sugar, sifted
grated zest of 1 lemon
1 tsp vanilla extract
pinch of sea salt
3–4 tbsp milk

1. Preheat the oven to 180°C/160°C fan/gas 4. Butter two 20cm (8in) round cake tins and line with baking parchment.

2. Using an electric whisk or stand mixer with whisk attachment, whisk the butter and sugar together on high speed until pale and creamy. Whisk in the eggs one by one until incorporated.

3. In another bowl, sift together the flour, baking powder, bicarbonate of soda and salt. Slowly mix in the milk, yoghurt, vanilla extract and lemon zest, then mix in the butter and egg mixture until fully combined.

4. Divide the mixture between the prepared cake tins and bake for 30–35 minutes, until a skewer comes out clean. If the tops are browning too quickly, cover with foil. Remove from the oven and leave in the tins to cool for 15 minutes, then turn out onto a wire rack to cool completely.

5. Meanwhile, make the icing. Using an electric whisk or stand mixer, beat the butter for a few minutes until light and fluffy. Gradually add the icing sugar, lemon zest, vanilla and salt until well combined. Finally add enough of the milk to make a smooth icing that still holds its shape.

6. Place one sponge on a serving plate and top with a third of the icing. Place the second sponge on top and cover the cake evenly with the remaining icing. Decorate with berries and flowers.

Tip
This sponge is made with milk and yoghurt, which keeps it incredibly moist and dense, but this means it should be stored in the fridge and eaten within three days.

CHOCOLATE ORANGE TART

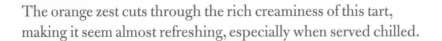

Best of
HOME COOK

The orange zest cuts through the rich creaminess of this tart, making it seem almost refreshing, especially when served chilled.

Serves 10
Prep time: 15 minutes, plus
    30 minutes chilling
Cook time: 50 minutes
VEGETARIAN

For the chocolate pastry
200g (7oz) plain flour, plus extra
    for dusting
3 tbsp cocoa powder
50g (2oz) icing sugar
grated zest of 1 orange
150g (5oz) unsalted butter, chilled
    and cut into small pieces
1 egg, beaten

For the filling
300ml (½ pint) double cream
grated zest of 2 oranges
150g (5oz) dark chocolate
    (70 per cent cocoa solids),
    broken into pieces
75g (3oz) milk chocolate,
    broken into pieces
1 tsp vanilla extract
1 tbsp triple sec
2 eggs, beaten

For the triple sec cream topping
300ml (½ pint) double cream
grated zest of 1 orange
1 tbsp triple sec
cocoa powder, for dusting

1. For the pastry, sift the flour, cocoa powder and icing sugar into the bowl of a food processor. Add the orange zest and chilled butter and blitz until the mixture resembles fine breadcrumbs. Alternatively, rub the butter into the flour using your fingertips. Add the egg and use your hands to bring the dough together until it forms a smooth ball. If it is still crumbly, add one or two drops of water, being careful not to overdo it. Flatten the ball, wrap in clingfilm and refrigerate for 30 minutes until well chilled but still pliable.

2. Preheat the oven to 200°C/180°C fan/gas 6.

3. Dust your work surface lightly with flour. Roll out the pastry to about 3mm (⅛in) thick and use to line a 24cm (9½in) round fluted loose-bottomed tart tin. Cover and chill for 15 minutes. Prick the base of the pastry all over with a fork, line with baking parchment, fill with baking beans and blind bake for 20 minutes. Remove the paper and beans and bake for a further 5 minutes until the pastry is cooked through and biscuity.

4. For the filling, put the cream and orange zest in a pan and cook over a medium heat until barely simmering. Add the dark and milk chocolate, vanilla and triple sec and stir until the chocolate has melted. Remove from the heat. Add the beaten eggs and immediately begin whisking very quickly until the mixture is smooth and thick. It is important you don't delay here, otherwise the eggs will scramble and the mixture will not be smooth.

5. Pour the mixture into the baked tart shell and bake for 12 minutes, until just set. Remove from the oven and leave to cool completely, then refrigerate for at least 1 hour or until well chilled. Alternatively, the tart can be served warm.

6. For the triple sec cream topping, put the cream, zest and liqueur in a bowl and whisk until soft peaks form. Slice the tart and serve with a dollop of the cream and a dusting of cocoa.

CHEESE, BUTTERNUT SQUASH & CUMIN SCONES

These savoury scones are incredibly moreish, and especially delicious hot from the oven. You can cook the dough as one large scone, ready to be torn into slices, or cut out and bake as individual scones.

Makes 8 scones
Prep time: 15 minutes
Cook time: 40 minutes
VEGETARIAN

300g (10½oz) butternut squash, peeled and de-seeded
50g (2oz) unsalted butter, chilled and cut into cubes
225g (8oz) plain flour, plus extra for dusting
¾ tsp sea salt
½ tsp freshly ground black pepper
2 tsp baking powder
2 tsp cumin seeds, plus extra for sprinkling (optional)
1 tsp sweet smoked paprika
½ tsp dried chilli flakes, plus extra for sprinkling (optional)
1 egg, beaten
Parmesan, for grating on top
salted butter, to serve

1. Preheat the oven to 220°c/200°c/gas 7 and line a baking sheet with baking parchment.

2. Weigh the prepared butternut squash: you will need 240g (8½oz), so you may need to peel and de-seed another chunk. Cut the squash into small pieces and cook in boiling water for 10–15 minutes until soft. Drain thoroughly in a sieve and return to the hot pan (not over the heat) to dry out for 5 minutes. Purée the squash in a food processor until smooth, then set aside.

3. Using your fingertips, rub the butter into the flour until the mixture resembles fine breadcrumbs. Mix in the salt, pepper, baking powder and spices. Stir in the squash purée to make a soft, sticky dough.

4. Dust your work surface with flour, tip the dough onto the work surface and lightly dust all over with flour. Gently shape the dough into a ball and transfer to the lined baking sheet, dusting with more flour if needed. Lightly flatten to make a rough circle, about 2cm (¾in) thick. Score the top of the dough into eight equal slices, like a pizza, ensuring you do not cut all the way through. Brush the top with the beaten egg.

5. Bake for 14–18 minutes until risen and golden. Grate some Parmesan over the top and sprinkle over a little more cumin seeds and chilli flakes, if you like. Serve warm with butter.

Tip
If you are vegetarian, look for vegetarian Italian-style hard cheese, as Parmesan is made with animal rennet.

Best of
HOME
COOK

STOTTIE CAKE

Originating in the north of England, this flat round bread is chewy and dense and perfect for a hearty sandwich or as an accompaniment to soup. A fantastic way to eat it, though, is while it is still warm, with plenty of salted butter and jam.

Makes 2 large loaves
Prep time: 30 minutes,
    plus 1½–2 hours rising
Cook time: 25 minutes
VEGETARIAN

1 × 7g sachet fast-action dried yeast
1 tsp caster sugar
200ml (7fl oz) warm water
550g (1¼lb) strong white bread flour,
    plus extra for dusting
2 tsp fine sea salt
100ml (3½fl oz) warm milk
100g (4oz) unsalted butter, melted
salted butter and jam, to serve

1. Put the yeast and sugar into a bowl and pour in the warm water. Give it a little stir and leave in a warm place for 10–15 minutes or until frothy.

2. Put the flour and salt into the bowl of a stand mixer, make a well in the centre, then pour in the yeasted water, warm milk and melted butter. Mix everything together until it forms a dough, then knead with a dough hook on low–medium speed for about 6 minutes, until smooth and stretchy. If you are kneading by hand, it will take about 12 minutes. Cover the bowl with a clean tea towel and leave to rise in a warm place (for example, beside a radiator) for 1–1½ hours, or until doubled in size.

3. Preheat the oven to 200°C/180°C fan/gas 6. Line two baking sheets with baking parchment.

4. Dust your worktop with a little flour. Knock the air out of the dough and divide into two equal pieces. Roll each piece into a flat round disc 2–3cm (about 1in) thick. Using your thumb, make an indentation in the centre of each disc. Transfer the discs to the prepared baking sheets and leave to rise for 30 minutes.

5. Bake for 15 minutes, then turn off the oven and leave for 10 minutes. Remove from the oven and leave to cool a little before serving.

PUDDINGS

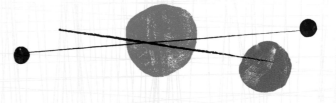

FRUITY RHUBARB & ALMOND CRUMBLE

A good crumble is hard to beat, the fruit soft and yielding, with a buttery, chewy topping. A warm embrace of a pudding.

Serves 6–8
Prep time: 10 minutes, plus cooling
Cook time: 35–40 minutes
VEGETARIAN

600g (1lb 5oz) forced rhubarb (see tip), trimmed and cut into 5cm (2in) chunks
4 plums or 300g (10½oz) other stone fruit (see tip), stoned and roughly chopped
120g (4½oz) golden caster sugar
grated zest of 1 lemon
100g (4oz) plain flour
75g (3oz) unsalted butter, chilled and cut into cubes, plus extra for greasing
75g (3oz) rolled oats
50g (2oz) flaked almonds
pinch of sea salt
ice cream or natural yoghurt, to serve

1. Preheat the oven to 200°c/180°c fan/gas 6. Butter a medium-sized baking dish, about 28 × 20cm (11 × 8in).

2. Combine the rhubarb with the plums/other stone fruit, half of the sugar, the lemon zest and three tablespoons of the flour. Transfer to the baking dish.

3. In a large bowl, rub the butter into the remaining flour until you have gravel-sized lumps. Mix in the oats, the remaining sugar, the flaked almonds and the salt. Scatter the crumble over the fruit and bake for 35–40 minutes until golden brown and bubbling. Leave to cool for 5 minutes, then serve with ice cream or yoghurt.

Tips
Forced rhubarb is sweeter than outdoor-grown, so if you use garden or field rhubarb you will need to add another two to three tablespoons of sugar.

You can use any stone fruit here in place of the plums (such as peaches, nectarines, apricots or cherries); apples and pears also work well with the rhubarb.

CHOCOLATE CHARLOTTE

This simplified version of the decadent dessert is a real crowd-pleaser. Great for dinner parties; make in advance to allow the mousse to set.

Serves 8
Prep time: 45 minutes, plus
   5 hours (minimum) chilling
VEGETARIAN

275–300g (10–10½oz) sponge fingers
   or savoiardi
350g (12oz) dark chocolate
   (70 per cent cocoa solids),
   broken into small pieces
150g (5oz) unsalted butter
7 eggs, separated
120g (4½oz) caster sugar
pinch of fine sea salt
150ml (¼ pint) double cream
1 tbsp triple sec (optional)

1. Line the base of a 20cm (8in) round deep springform tin with baking parchment.

2. Trim one end off 26 of the sponge fingers, so that they stand upright. Use these fingers to line the sides of the tin, sugared side facing out, packing them closely so there are no gaps. You may need to trim the last finger so that it fits in exactly. If necessary, brush the fingers with a little water to help them stay in place.

3. Take some more sponge fingers and line the base of the cake tin, again breaking some of them to fill in the gaps.

4. Melt 300g (10½oz) of the chocolate with the butter in a heatproof bowl over a pan of barely simmering water. Leave to cool for a few minutes.

5. Using an electric whisk or a stand mixer, whisk the egg yolks and 70g of the sugar together until pale, thick and creamy. Slowly fold in the melted chocolate and butter mixture.

6. Ensuring the bowl and beaters are clean and grease-free, use an electric whisk or a stand mixer to whisk the egg whites with the salt until they form soft peaks, then whisk in the remaining sugar to form stiff, glossy peaks. Gently fold the whites into the chocolate a few tablespoons at a time, until fully combined.

7. Put half of the chocolate mousse into the lined cake tin. Top with more sponge fingers, breaking some of them to fill the gaps. Pour the remaining mousse on top and smooth with the back of a spoon. Cover and refrigerate for at least 5 hours or overnight.

8. When ready to serve, whisk the cream and triple sec (if using) until soft peaks form. Spoon the whipped cream on top of the charlotte to form a dome. Unclip the sides of the tin and run a palette knife under the base to remove the lining. Place on a serving plate. Melt the remaining chocolate and drizzle over the top. Serve immediately.

STICKY TOFFEE PUDDINGS
WITH GINGER SAUCE

A wonderful British classic given a little twist with a ginger sauce. While sublime fresh from the oven, these can be made in advance and warmed through before serving. Cool quickly but completely and store in an airtight container for up to two days.

Best of
HOME
COOK

Serves 8
Prep time: 15 minutes, plus cooling
Cook time: 30 minutes
VEGETARIAN

225g (8oz) pitted Medjool dates
100ml (3½fl oz) water
100ml (3½fl oz) whole milk
100g (4oz) unsalted butter, softened, plus extra for greasing
150g (5oz) soft light brown sugar
2 tbsp blackstrap molasses or black treacle
3 eggs
2 tsp vanilla extract
pinch of sea salt
175g (6oz) plain flour
1 tsp baking powder
½ tsp bicarbonate of soda

For the sticky toffee sauce
100g (4oz) soft light brown sugar
100g (4oz) salted butter
120ml (4½fl oz) double cream, plus extra to serve
1 tbsp finely chopped crystallised ginger (optional)
2 thick slices of fresh ginger (optional)
1 tbsp blackstrap molasses or black treacle

1. Preheat the oven to 200°C/180°C fan/gas 6. Butter eight mini pudding or dariole moulds and line the bases with discs of baking parchment.

2. Roughly chop the dates and put them in a pan with the water and bring to the boil. Reduce the heat and simmer for 3–5 minutes until the dates are completely soft.

3. Place the date mixture in a food processor and blitz until smooth. Add the milk, butter, sugar, molasses, eggs, vanilla extract and salt and blitz again until well combined. Sift and fold in the flour, baking powder and bicarbonate of soda.

4. Divide the mixture between the prepared moulds. Bake for 20–25 minutes or until risen and just set; a skewer should come out clean. If they are beginning to burn, cover with foil. Remove from the oven and leave to cool for 5 minutes, then trim off the rounded tops, so the puddings will sit flat when turned out. Gently remove from the tins and turn out onto serving plates.

5. While the puddings are cooking, make the sauce. Place the sugar, butter, cream and both gingers (if using) in a pan over a medium heat and cook until the sugar has dissolved. Add the molasses or treacle and cook for another 4–6 minutes, stirring all the time, until the mixture has thickened a little and darkened in colour. Remove the slices of fresh ginger.

6. Serve the puddings with the toffee sauce and some double cream drizzled over.

BANOFFEE CHOCOLATE PIE

This indulgent twist on banoffee pie pairs bananas with rich dark chocolate and sweet caramel for a match made in dessert heaven. If you prefer a more traditional pie, see the tip below.

Serves 12
Prep time: 30 minutes, plus cooling
VEGETARIAN

For the base
300g (10½oz) dark chocolate
    digestive biscuits
100g (4oz) salted butter, melted,
    plus extra for greasing

For the filling
100g (4oz) dark chocolate
    (70 per cent cocoa solids),
    broken into small pieces
350g (12oz) caramel or
    dulce de leche
pinch of sea salt

For the topping
300ml (½ pint) double cream
4 bananas, peeled and sliced
cocoa powder and/or grated dark
    chocolate, for dusting

1. Butter a 23cm (9in) round springform tin.

2. To make the base, put the biscuits into a food processor and blitz until ground to a powder. Transfer to a bowl and combine with the melted butter. Press the mixture firmly and evenly over the base of the cake tin. Cover and place in the freezer for 10 minutes to set.

3. Meanwhile, to make the filling, melt the chocolate in a heatproof bowl over a pan of barely simmering water, ensuring the base of the bowl does not come into contact with the water. Once the chocolate has melted, add the caramel and salt and stir over the heat until fully combined. Pour the caramel mixture onto the biscuit base, spread evenly and leave to cool, then cover and place in the freezer for 10 minutes to set.

4. Whisk the cream until soft peaks form. Cover the caramel layer with most of the sliced banana. Dollop the whipped cream on top, scatter over the remaining sliced banana and dust with cocoa powder and/or grated chocolate. Serve immediately or cover and keep in the fridge until ready to eat.

Tip
For a more traditional banoffee pie, use plain digestive biscuits for the base, omit the chocolate from the filling and increase the caramel to 400g (14oz).

STRAWBERRY & ALMOND ROULADE

Adding ground almonds to the meringue gives the roulade a delightful chewiness, while the muddled strawberries swirled through the filling are a perfect foil to the rich cream.

Best of
HOME
COOK

Serves 6–8
Prep time: 35 minutes, plus cooling
    and chilling
Cook time: 30 minutes
VEGETARIAN

vegetable oil, for greasing
6 egg whites
320g (11oz) caster sugar,
    plus 2 tbsp for dusting
¼ tsp white wine vinegar
1 tsp cornflour, sifted
50g (2oz) ground almonds
pinch of sea salt
2 tbsp flaked almonds
300ml (½ pint) double cream
300g (10½oz) strawberries, hulled,
    plus extra to serve
3 tbsp icing sugar, plus extra to serve

1. Preheat the oven to 200°c/180°c fan/gas 6. Grease a 34 × 22cm (13 × 8½in) Swiss roll tin and line with baking parchment, ensuring the edge of the paper fits exactly into the tin.

2. Ensuring the bowl is clean and grease-free, whisk the egg whites in a stand mixer or using an electric whisk until they form stiff peaks. Gradually add the caster sugar, a few tablespoons at a time, whisking continuously until you have stiff, glossy peaks. This may take up to 6–8 minutes. Fold in the vinegar, cornflour, ground almonds and salt.

3. Transfer the mixture to the prepared tin and smooth out using the back of a spoon. Bake for 8 minutes until golden, then turn down the oven to 160°c/140°c fan/gas 3 and bake for another 20 minutes until just firm and slightly springy to the touch.

4. Shortly before the meringue has finished cooking, scatter the flaked almonds on a baking sheet and roast in the oven for 3–4 minutes, until golden and aromatic.

5. Place a large sheet of baking parchment on your work surface and dust liberally with the remaining two tablespoons of caster sugar. Carefully invert the meringue onto the parchment. The easiest way to do this is to place a thin chopping board, roughly the size of the baking tin, on top of the meringue, invert the meringue onto the board, peel off the baking paper and then carefully slide the meringue off the board onto the sugar-dusted baking parchment. Score a line 2cm (¾in) in from the edge along one long side of the meringue, ensuring you do not cut all the way through. Leave to cool for 10 minutes while you make the filling.

Recipe continues overleaf

6. Whisk the cream until soft peaks form. Using a fork, lightly mash half of the strawberries, so they still have a little bit of texture but have released their juice. Stir the mashed strawberries through the whipped cream and spread the mixture over the meringue, leaving a 1–2cm (½–¾in) border all round. Using the baking parchment, roll up the meringue (the line you scored earlier will help you to roll it up tightly). Wrap the parchment around the roll, leave it seam side down on a serving platter and refrigerate for at least 30 minutes until well chilled.

7. Meanwhile, put the remaining strawberries into a food processor, together with the icing sugar, and blitz until smooth. Pass through a fine sieve into a bowl and set aside.

8. To serve, unwrap the roulade and arrange some strawberries on top, scatter over the almonds and dust with icing sugar. Serve immediately, drizzled with strawberry sauce.

PEARS IN MARSALA
WITH ICE CREAM

Marsala is a dark, sweet dessert wine produced in Sicily, used here to poach pears until they become tender and soak up all the delicious flavour. If you have any poaching liquid left over, keep it in the fridge and use to drizzle over ice cream or any other pudding.

Serves 6
Prep time: 15 minutes
Cook time: 35–50 minutes
VEGETARIAN
VEGAN – omitting the ice cream

6 firm pears, such as Conference
1 orange
1 lemon
550ml (19fl oz) Marsala
75g (3oz) golden caster sugar
1 cinnamon stick
1 vanilla pod, slit lengthways and
    seeds scraped out
3 bay leaves
vanilla ice cream, to serve

1. Peel the pears, but leave their stalks intact. Cut a thin slice off the base of each pear, so that it can stand upright for serving. Carefully peel the zest off the orange and lemon, trying not to remove any pith.

2. Put the Marsala, sugar, cinnamon, vanilla pod and seeds, bay leaves and citrus peel into a pan (with a lid) that is just large enough to hold all the pears. Test out the size of the pan before proceeding if you are unsure.

3. Place the pan over a high heat and bring to the boil. Immediately reduce the heat to medium–low, add the pears, and pour in enough water to raise the level of the liquid to almost reach the top of the pears, but no more than 200ml (7fl oz). Cover with the lid and simmer very gently for 25–35 minutes – this will depend on the pears you are using – until a small sharp knife glides easily into the thickest part of a pear.

4. Once the pears are tender, use a slotted spoon to transfer them to a plate, and set aside. Remove and discard the cinnamon stick, vanilla pod, bay leaves and citrus peel. Bring the liquid to the boil and reduce for 10–15 minutes until it is slightly thicker.

5. Serve the pears with the ice cream and some of the cooking liquid drizzled over.

Tip
To make this in advance, leave the pears to cool while you reduce the poaching liquid, leave the liquid to cool, then store together in a bowl in the fridge. Reheat just before serving.

BUTTERNUT SQUASH TARTE TATIN

The classic French apple tarte Tatin is reimagined here with butternut squash, which works very well in a sweet context.

Serves 6–8
Prep time: 20 minutes
Cook time: 1 hour
VEGETARIAN

600g (1lb 5oz) butternut squash
2 tbsp olive oil
pinch of sea salt
2 tbsp runny honey
40g (1½oz) golden caster sugar
1 tbsp cold water
40g (1½oz) salted butter
½ tsp ground nutmeg
2 tsp ground cinnamon
plain flour, for dusting
250g (9oz) ready-rolled puff pastry

To serve
200g (7oz) fresh custard
grated zest of 1 lemon

1. Preheat the oven to 200°C/180°C fan/gas 6.

2. Peel the squash and cut in half lengthways. Remove the seeds and cut the squash into 5mm (¼in) slices. Toss the squash with the olive oil and arrange in a single layer on one or two baking sheets. Season with a pinch of salt and roast for 15 minutes until golden but still a little firm to the touch. Remove and set aside.

3. Put the honey, sugar and water into a heavy-based 20cm (8cm) ovenproof frying pan and place over a medium heat. Cook gently, stirring now and again, until you have a golden caramel. Stir in the butter, nutmeg and cinnamon, then remove from the heat.

4. Arrange the butternut squash slices in an overlapping fan pattern over the base of the pan: take great care as the caramel will be extremely hot. Cook for another 3–5 minutes until the syrup is deeply caramelised. Remove from the heat.

5. On a worktop dusted with flour, cut out a disc of puff pastry that is 2cm (¾in) larger than the pan you are using. Position the pastry over the butternut squash and tuck the edges down around the side, using the tip of a knife to ease it into place. Prick a few small holes in the pastry to allow steam to escape.

6. Bake for 30–35 minutes until the pastry is golden and crisp. Remove from the oven and leave to cool for 2 minutes, but no longer, otherwise the caramel will stick to the pan, making it difficult to remove the tart. Place a large plate on top of the pan and, in one swift movement, invert the tarte Tatin onto the plate, taking care as the caramel will still be very hot.

7. Mix together the custard and lemon zest and serve alongside the tarte Tatin.

ROAST PLUM BAKE
WITH STREUSEL CRUMBLE

This deconstructed crumble allows the plums to shine like jewels
on top, while the bed of streusel soaks up all the delicious juices.

Serves 4
Prep time: 15 minutes
Cook time: 25–30 minutes
VEGETARIAN

6 plums, halved and stoned
2 tbsp salted butter
3 tbsp demerara sugar

For the streusel crumble
100g (4oz) salted butter, chilled
    and cut into cubes
100g (4oz) plain flour
100g (4oz) demerara sugar
100g (4oz) flaked almonds

For the amaretto cream (optional)
200ml (7fl oz) double cream
3 tbsp icing sugar, sifted
3 tbsp amaretto

1. Preheat the oven to 200°C/180°C fan/gas 6. Line a baking sheet
with baking parchment.

2. For the amaretto cream, place all the ingredients in a bowl and
whisk until soft peaks form. Cover and refrigerate until needed.

3. For the crumble, rub the butter into the flour until the mixture
resembles breadcrumbs, then stir in the sugar and flaked almonds.
Transfer to the lined baking sheet and set aside.

4. For the plums, melt the butter in a large frying pan over
a medium heat. Add the plums, cut side down, and fry for
2–3 minutes until barely golden. Transfer the plums to the
baking sheet, sitting them skin side down on top of the crumble.
Sprinkle the sugar over the plums.

5. Bake for 20–25 minutes, stirring the crumble once or twice,
until golden brown and crisp and the plums are soft. Leave to
cool for a few minutes, then serve with the amaretto cream.

Tip
If you prefer, you can serve this with ice cream instead of the
amaretto cream.

MINI CHOCOLATE
MOLTEN PUDDINGS

These individual self-saucing chocolate puddings are perfect for
a dinner party. They are very easy to make, but you do need to time
the cooking to ensure you achieve the gooey molten centre.

Serves 8
Prep time: 20 minutes, plus cooling
Cook time: 9–10 minutes
VEGETARIAN

150g (5oz) unsalted butter, plus
    extra for greasing
cocoa powder, for dusting
225g (8oz) dark chocolate
    (70 per cent cocoa solids),
    broken into small pieces
3 eggs
3 egg yolks
160g (5½oz) caster sugar
110ml (4fl oz) Irish cream liqueur
50g (2oz) plain flour
200ml (7fl oz) double cream

1. Preheat the oven to 200°c/180°c fan/gas 6. Butter eight dariole moulds or ramekins and dust with cocoa powder.

2. Melt the butter and chocolate in a heatproof bowl over a pan of barely simmering water, ensuring the base of the bowl does not come into contact with the water.

3. Meanwhile, using an electric whisk or stand mixer with whisk attachment, whisk the eggs, egg yolks and sugar together until pale, thick and creamy: this may take 4–5 minutes. Stir in 50ml (2fl oz) of the Irish cream liqueur and the melted chocolate and butter mixture. Sift and fold in the flour.

4. Divide the mixture between the prepared moulds and bake for 9–10 minutes, until they have a firm crust, but are still obviously soft in the centre. Take care not to overcook them. Remove from the oven and leave to cool for 5 minutes.

5. While they are cooking, put the double cream and the remaining Irish cream liqueur into a bowl and whisk until thick and just holding its shape. Turn the puddings out onto serving plates and serve immediately, with the whipped cream.

Tip
Simply omit the Irish cream liqueur if you prefer an alcohol-free pudding.

PASSION FRUIT & LIME POSSETS WITH GINGER SHORTBREAD CRUMBLE

Decadent, rich and creamy possets with a refreshing note from the lime, passion fruit and ginger, and a gentle crunch from the crumble. The perfect ending to an evening meal.

Serves 4
Prep time: 15 minutes, plus cooling
    and 2 hours (minimum) chilling
Cook time: 20–25 minutes
VEGETARIAN

400ml (14fl oz) double cream
75g (3oz) caster sugar
grated zest and juice of 2 limes
6 ripe passion fruit, halved and
    pulp scooped out
1 tsp finely chopped stem ginger

For the ginger shortbread crumble
85g (3½oz) plain flour
1 tsp ground ginger
60g (2½oz) unsalted butter,
    chilled and cut into cubes
45g (1½oz) caster sugar

1. Heat the cream and sugar in a pan and bring to the boil. Immediately reduce the heat and simmer for 3 minutes, then remove from the heat.

2. Stir in most of the lime zest, all the juice, the passion fruit pulp and stem ginger and mix well. Divide the mixture between four small glasses or bowls. Leave to cool completely, then cover and refrigerate for at least 2 hours until chilled and set.

3. Preheat the oven to 190°C/170°C fan/gas 5. Line a baking sheet with baking parchment.

4. For the ginger shortbread crumble, rub the flour, ground ginger, butter and sugar together in a small bowl, until the mixture resembles breadcrumbs. Transfer to the lined baking sheet and bake for 15–20 minutes, stirring once or twice, until lightly golden. Remove and leave to cool.

5. To serve, sprinkle the crumble over the possets and scatter over the remaining lime zest.

Best of
HOME
COOK

RASPBERRY & PISTACHIO PAVLOVA

There's a surprise layer of raspberries and cream filling inside this spectacular 'double' pavlova. The meringue base can be made in advance and stored in an airtight container for two or three days, but do not assemble the pavlova until the last moment.

Serves 8–10
Prep time: 30 minutes, plus cooling
Cook time: 1 hour
VEGETARIAN

4 egg whites, at room temperature
250g (9oz) caster sugar
¼ tsp vanilla extract
1 tsp white wine vinegar
1 tsp cornflour, sifted
pinch of fine sea salt

For the topping
400ml (14fl oz) double cream
2 tbsp caster sugar
250g (9oz) full-fat natural yoghurt
200g (7oz) raspberries
50g (2oz) raw shelled pistachio nuts, roughly chopped
small handful of mint leaves
icing sugar, for dusting

1. Preheat the oven to 150°C/130°C fan/gas 2. Line two baking sheets with baking parchment.

2. Ensuring the bowl is clean and grease-free, whisk the egg whites in a stand mixer or using an electric whisk until they begin to form stiff peaks. Gradually add the caster sugar, one tablespoon at a time, whisking continuously until you have stiff, glossy peaks. This may take up to 6 minutes. Whisk in the vanilla extract, vinegar, cornflour and salt.

3. Using a metal spoon, spread half the mixture onto one of the prepared baking sheets, shaping it into a circle approximately 20cm (8in) in diameter, making a slight dip in the middle. Repeat with the remaining mixture on the second baking sheet. Bake the meringues for 1 hour, then turn off the oven, leaving the meringues in the oven for 20 minutes. Remove from the oven and leave to cool completely.

4. Whisk the cream with the caster sugar until soft peaks form. Stir in the yoghurt. Place one disc of meringue on a serving plate, top with half the cream mixture and a handful of the raspberries. Place the second disc of meringue on top, spoon over the remaining cream mixture and scatter over the remaining raspberries, the pistachio nuts and mint leaves. Dust with a little icing sugar and serve immediately.

Tip
Feel free to use different berries, or a combination.

CAMBRIDGE BURNT CREAM
WITH CHERRIES

Whether the Cambridge burnt cream was invented before the more famous French crème brûlée is up for debate. Regardless, this creamy custard topped with crisp caramelised sugar is a true classic, loved by all. The cherries offer a lovely fresh contrast to the rich cream.

Serves 6–8
Prep time: 20 minutes, plus cooling
Cook time: 40–50 minutes
VEGETARIAN

450ml (¾ pint) double cream
150ml (¼ pint) whole milk
1 vanilla pod, slit lengthways and
    seeds scraped out
6 egg yolks
100g (4oz) caster sugar
demerara sugar, or extra caster sugar,
    for the topping
150g (5oz) cherries, halved
    and stoned

1. Preheat the oven to 150°C/130°C fan/gas 2. Place six to eight ramekins in a large, deep baking tin.

2. Pour the cream and milk into a pan and add the vanilla pod and seeds. Place over a medium–high heat and bring to a gentle simmer and cook for 10 minutes. Remove the pan from the heat and discard the vanilla pod.

3. Leave the cream and milk to infuse for 5–10 minutes while you gently but evenly combine the egg yolks and caster sugar in a bowl. Pour the cream mixture over the egg yolk mixture and stir to combine, then strain through a fine sieve into a jug.

4. Divide the mixture between the ramekins. Boil a full kettle of water, then put the baking tin into the oven and pour in enough boiling water to come halfway up the side of the ramekins. Bake for 35–40 minutes until just set but still a little wobbly in the centre.

5. Remove the ramekins from the baking tin and leave to cool completely. At this point they can be covered and kept in the fridge for up to two days.

6. When ready to serve, sprinkle a generous and even layer of demerara sugar over the custard, then caramelise with a blowtorch or place the ramekins under a very hot grill until the sugar turns a deep, dark, almost burnt caramel colour. Serve immediately with some cherries on top.

APPLE CHARLOTTE PUDDING

This wonderful combination of apples with caramel, butterscotch sauce and Chantilly cream is perfect for a Sunday pud.

Serves 6
Prep time: 15–20 minutes,
    plus cooling
Cook time: 1¼ hours
VEGETARIAN

120g (4½oz) caster sugar
3 tbsp water
6 Cox's apples, peeled, cored and
    chopped into 1cm (½in) pieces
2 tbsp Calvados
juice of 1 orange
½ tsp ground cinnamon
100g (4oz) salted butter, melted,
    plus extra for greasing
6 slices of white bread

For the butterscotch sauce
60g (2½oz) caster sugar
4 tbsp water
20g (¾oz) unsalted butter
200ml (7fl oz) double cream

For the Chantilly cream (optional)
200ml (7fl oz) double cream
2 tbsp icing sugar, sifted
a few drops of vanilla extract

1. Preheat the oven to 200°c/180°c fan/gas 6. Butter a 1 litre (1¾ pint) pudding basin.

2. Put the sugar and water into a pan (with a lid) over a low heat. Cook gently until the sugar has dissolved and is light golden.

3. Add the chopped apples to the caramel, stir and then add the Calvados, orange juice, cinnamon and 20g of the melted butter. Cover and bring to the boil, cook for 5 minutes, then remove the lid and cook for another 10–15 minutes until all the liquid has evaporated and the apple is soft. Remove from the heat and set the cooked apple aside to cool.

4. Flatten the bread slices slightly with a rolling pin and remove the crusts. Dip the bread in the remaining melted butter. Use about four slices of the bread to line the base and sides of the basin, overlapping the bread slightly to ensure there are no gaps.

5. Spoon the cooked apple into the bread-lined basin. Cover with the remaining bread and press down to seal, pinching the edges of the bread together.

6. Put the pudding basin on a baking sheet and bake for 35–40 minutes until deep golden brown and crisp on top. Leave to cool for 5 minutes, then carefully invert onto a serving plate.

7. While the pudding is cooking, make the butterscotch sauce. Put the sugar and water into a pan over a low heat. Bring to the boil, then simmer until the sugar is a dark golden caramel. Whisk in the butter, stir in the cream and continue to simmer for 5 minutes, stirring all the time, until the sauce is creamy and golden brown. Remove from the heat.

8. For the Chantilly cream, whisk the cream, icing sugar and vanilla extract together until stiff peaks form.

9. To serve, pour the sauce over the pudding. The Chantilly cream can be served on the side for guests to help themselves.

BERRY TRIFLE

This old-school classic is very easy to make, especially as you can buy good-quality fresh custard in supermarkets. It is best served after an hour or two, just as the flavours are getting to know one another, but can be made in advance and stored in the fridge overnight.

Serves 8
Prep time: 25 minutes, plus cooling
    and 1 hour (minimum) chilling
Cook time: 10 minutes
VEGETARIAN

500g (1lb 2oz) fresh or frozen
    (defrosted) mixed berries
75g (3oz) caster sugar
200g (7oz) sponge fingers
    or savoiardi
5 tbsp sweet sherry
175g (6oz) amaretti biscuits
750g (1lb 10oz) fresh cold custard
300ml (½ pint) double cream
2 tsp vanilla extract
2–3 tbsp pomegranate seeds
    (optional)
100g (4oz) fresh blackberries
20g (¾oz) flaked almonds

1. Put the mixed berries and sugar in a pan over a medium–low heat, lightly mashing together until they release some of their juices, then increase the heat and bring to the boil. Reduce the heat and simmer rapidly for 10 minutes until slightly reduced. Leave to cool completely.

2. Neatly cover the base of a large trifle bowl (about 3.5 litres/ 6 pints) with the sponge fingers, so that they are visible at the sides of the bowl. Stir the sherry into the cooled berry mixture and spread it over the sponge fingers. Layer the amaretti on top so that they are also visible at the sides of the bowl, then pour the custard on top.

3. Whisk the double cream with the vanilla extract until soft peaks form, then spoon over the custard. Cover and chill in the fridge for at least an hour or overnight.

4. When ready to serve, scatter over the pomegranate seeds (if using), blackberries and flaked almonds.

Tips
If you want to avoid alcohol, use orange juice instead of the sherry.

You can use cubes of Madeira cake instead of the sponge fingers or amaretti biscuits, if you prefer.

Family
→ Rules ←
Love each other
ALWAYS TRY YOUR BEST
Tell the truth | Laugh a lot!
Always SHARE Your hugs
Play
lots &
LOTS of
games
DREAM
BIG
★

MEET THE CONTESTANTS

Katie

Dipa

Cyrus

Trevor

Pippa

Fiona

Josie

Philip

Q

Tobi

INDEX

ACKNOWLEDGEMENTS

KEO Films is the multi-award-winning production company behind innovative, ethical content including the BAFTA-winning 'Exodus: Our Journey to Europe' for BBC Two; 'Eden' and 'The Romanians are Coming' for Channel 4; the Academy Award-nominated documentary 'Exit Through the Gift Shop'; Hugh Fearnley-Whittingstall's 'War on Waste'; and the hugely successful River Cottage brand. Keo Films are based out of London, Glasgow and Bristol.

Jordan Bourke is a chef, food writer and best-selling author. He has won the best cookbook awards at the distinguished Observer Food Monthly Awards and Fortnum & Mason Awards. His work has featured in the *The Times*, the *Sunday Times*, the *Guardian* and the *Observer* and he has appeared on Channel 4's 'Sunday Brunch', BBC One's 'Saturday Kitchen' and he is a panelist on Radio 4's 'The Kitchen Cabinet'. Jordan lives in London with his wife and young son.

Instagram @jordanbourke | Twitter @jordanbourk

Jordan's Thanks:

It was a real joy working on this book, and this was largely down to the wonderful team who made it all happen: Lizzy and Charlotte at the Publishers; my editor Emily; copy editor Maggie; the designer Clare; the shoot team led by photographer Kim; the prop stylist Linda; and food stylist Sian and her assistant Megan, who kindly came in to cover me on the last few shoot days. Thanks also to my assistant Fiona, agent Claudia, Keo Films, the BBC and everyone working on the show.

Keo's Thanks:

Thanks to Antony Topping at Greene and Heaton, and Lizzy and her team at Ebury for their constant support in making this book happen. Thanks, too, to Lou Plank for wrangling the myriad of PR requirements. And we are especially grateful to the following people who put their hearts, souls and long, long hours into the programme: Claire Nosworthy, Andrew Palmer, Matt Cole, Clare Paterson, David Brindley, Catherine Catton, Antonia Lloyd, Martha Swales, Alice Binks, Rosa Brough, Hannah Weetman, Maddy Allen, Trevor Lopez De Vergara and Jade Miller-Robinson.

Cookery Notes:

Both metric and imperial measurements are used in this book. Follow one set of measurements throughout a recipe, not a mixture, as they are not interchangeable.

All spoon measurements are level. 1 teaspoon = 5 ml; 1 tablespoon = 15 ml.

All eggs are organic and medium unless otherwise specified.

Some recipes use raw or very lightly cooked eggs. The elderly, infants, pregnant women and anyone with an impaired immune system should avoid these recipes.

10 9 8 7 6 5 4 3 2 1

BBC Books, an imprint of Ebury Publishing
20 Vauxhall Bridge Road,
London SW1V 2SA

BBC Books is part of the Penguin Random House group of companies whose addresses can be found at global.penguinrandomhouse.com

Penguin
Random House
UK

Copyright © Keo Films Limited, 2018
© Woodlands Book Limited, 2018

Jordan Bourke has asserted his right to be identified as the author of this Work in accordance with the Copyright, Designs and Patents Act 1988

This book is published to accompany the television series entitled 'Britain's Best Home Cook', first broadcast on BBC One in 2018. 'Britain's Best Home Cook' is a Keo Films production.

First published by BBC Books in 2018

www.penguin.co.uk

A CIP catalogue record for this book is available from the British Library

ISBN 9781785943409

Colour origination by Altaimage, London

Printed and bound by Firmengruppe APPL, aprinta druck, Wemding, Germany

Penguin Random House is committed to a sustainable future for our business, our readers and our planet. This book is made from Forest Stewardship Council® certified paper.

MIX
Paper from
responsible sources
FSC® C018179

EXECUTIVE PRODUCERS:
Claire Nosworthy, Andrew Palmer, Matt Cole, Clare Paterson

COMMISSIONERS FOR THE BBC:
David Brindley, Catherine Catton

SERIES PRODUCER: *Antonia Lloyd*

FOOD PRODUCER: *Martha Swales*

CHALLENGE PRODUCER: *Alice Binks*

CHALLENGE ASSISTANT PRODUCERS:
Rosa Brough, Hannah Weetman

HEAD OF PRODUCTION: *Maddy Allen*

PRODUCTION EXECUTIVE:
Trevor Lopez De Vergara

PRODUCTION MANAGER:
Jade Miller-Robinson

PUBLISHING DIRECTOR: *Lizzy Gray*

PROJECT EDITOR: *Emily Preece-Morrison*

DESIGN: *Clare Skeats*

PHOTOGRAPHER: *Kim Lightbody*

COVER PHOTOGRAPHER: *Ray Burmiston*

RECIPE DEVELOPMENT: *Jordan Bourke*

FOOD STYLISTS: *Jordan Bourke and Sian Henley*

FOOD STYLING ASSISTANTS:
Fiona Giles and Megan Davies

PROP STYLIST: *Linda Berlin*

COPY EDITOR: *Maggie Ramsay*

INDEXER: *Vanessa Bird*

PRODUCTION: *Rebecca Jones*